THE SPIRIT AND THE WORD

"This little book is a series of meditations on the life of the Spirit of Jesus in us. They are reflections which have grown out of my reading and teaching of the Bible, my experience of the spiritual life, and my ministry to others. If the book has a charismatic flavor, it is because the charismatic discovery has been a significant turning point in my life.

". . . If this groping attempt to understand helps the reader in any measure (to) know himself and the Lord better, it will have been well worth the effort."

—George T. Montague

"RIDING THE WIND is one of the finest books I have read to learn 'the ways of the Spirit'. The writer knows how to be personal and doctrinal at the same time. He makes Scripture alive. The reader can feel Father Montague's love for the Lord and His Mother, his faith in the power of the Spirit and his confidence 'that the age of miracles is not past'."

—Cardinal Leo Jozeph Suenens

Riding
the
Wind

Learning the Ways of the Spirit
By George T. Montague, S.M.

PILLAR BOOKS  NEW YORK

Nihil Obstat: Reverend Norman F. Josaitis

Imprimatur: Most Reverend Alexander M. Zaleski
                    Bishop of Lansing

RIDING THE WIND

A PILLAR BOOK
Published by arrangement with Word of Life

Pillar Books edition published January 1977

ISBN: 0-89129-256-X

Library of Congress Catalog Card Number: 76-40747

Copyright © 1974 Word of Life

Printed in the United States of America

PILLAR BOOKS
Pyramid Publications
(Harcourt Brace Jovanovich, Inc.)
757 Third Avenue
New York, New York 10017
U.S.A.

Contents

Invitation

This little book is a series of meditations on the life of the Spirit of Jesus in us. They are reflections which have grown out of my reading and teaching of the Bible, my experience of the spiritual life, and my ministry to others. If the book has a charismatic flavor, it is because the charismatic discovery has been a significant turning point in my life. And yet, my hope is that even for those who have not had the same experience, there may be enough of the human and the Christian with which they may identify that they will find here refreshment and invitation to grow. The mixture of the old and the new will, I hope, appeal to the Christian whom Jesus describes as a "scribe become a disciple of the kingdom of heaven . . . who knows how to bring out of his storeroom things new and old" (Matt. 13:51).

Several reasons impel me to begin this book with a chapter on my personal salvation history. First, biblically speaking, our God is a God of persons, the God of Abraham, of Isaac, of Jacob, of Jesus Christ. He is also the God of Paul and Peter, of Mary Magdalene and Zacchaeus. The Lord reveals himself in the lives of his people: "God chose to reveal his Son in me" (Gal. 1:14). If this is true, then each of us has in his own experience the raw materials for a personal salvation history. And hence a reflection in faith on my life can enable me to say, "O God, you are *my* God" (Psalm 63:1).

Secondly, for persons with an intellectual bent and training like myself, it is all too easy to talk about God and the life of the Spirit to the neglect of personal experience. Preaching and teaching all too easily can become a matter of telling others what they should do—

and for the *why* giving every other reason than the most gripping one; "because this is what happened to me."

Thirdly, I am convinced that despite a scholar's best efforts to be objective, he cannot escape the subjectivity of his own experience and the immense influence it has even on what he looks for and finds in his research. Particularly is this true in the area of religion. The most honest thing for me to do is to confess the experience in which I stand and to allow the reader to judge for himself how much "objectivity" there is in the rest of the things I say. In this series of meditations I have tried to respect the Scriptures I have used and not to make them say more than they are saying. But the reader should know that my reflections come as much out of my experience of the Christian life as they do out of the scholar's "detached" view of the biblical text.

Fourthly, I am further convinced that to meet Jesus in the deep encounter of faith and the Spirit is to experience a healing of the memories. Augustine is most remembered for his *Confessions*. These are less a confession of guilt than a confession of praise for the Lord's work in the life of Augustine. Accepting the Lord meant for Augustine also accepting himself and his history in a healing way. Teresa of Avila and John of the Cross wrote extensively about the healing of the memories. If their words were not sufficient, then experience would convince me that the minister is as effective in healing others as he has himself been healed. And this means allowing himself to be loved and touched in his memories. It means accepting himself and his history both as his own and as the Lord's.

And so I begin by sharing my own life experience. It is a mystery which I do not pretend to fully understand. "For now we see in a mirror dimly, but then face to face. Now I know in part; then I shall understand fully, even as I have been fully understood" (1 Cor. 13:12). If this groping attempt to understand helps the reader in any measure know himself and the Lord better, it will have been well worth the effort.

March, 1973

CHAPTER ONE

Riding the Wind

I was born on a Texas ranch in the summer of 1929. The stock market crashed shortly thereafter. This sequence of events has always amused me, and I used to remind my mother that my birth was so important that after it the whole country went into a postnatal depression.

That Texas ranch would have a lot to do with shaping my roots. I learned to love the moist mornings and the smell of the fields at harvest time. On a summer day, when I was not rounding up livestock or squirrel-hunting with my dog in the river bottom, I found nothing more fascinating than lying in the shade of an oak tree and letting myself be mesmerized by the endless armada of cumulus clouds that floated through the skies. Sometimes I would be distracted by swirling specks I knew to be a flock of buzzards riding tireless circles on the high winds. Coming home with my father at the end of the day, I learned to pause before a symphony of color as the sun set ablaze the western sky before dipping out of sight behind the distant hills. And at night I never tired of drinking in the skyful of brilliant stars. I never bothered to learn their names, I just let them create in me a sense of wonder and awe.

But often, my contact with nature produced not exhilaration but a mysterious melancholy and nostalgia. The feeling puzzled me then as it does even now. Perhaps it was the "otherness" of the universe I felt, an otherness which I could never fathom nor possess. The stars and the clouds had been there for millions of years before me, and they would continue their timeless journeying when I was no longer there. They did not appear to notice me when I came to admire them, nor did they say good-bye when I had to leave. They seemed to be pursuing some elusive goal with relentless and undivided attention, like the shoemaker I once stopped to watch through a window—he took no notice of my presence, nor did he seem diminished by my absence when I left. So perhaps the greatest lesson I learned from nature was that my heart was made for something more.

My lifestory has been the search for that something more.

Part of that more was my family. My father was a man full of life in every ounce of his six-foot, two-hundred-and-eighty-pound frame. He filled any room he entered, and when he stood on Main Street in front of the O.S.T. Cafe, as he was wont to do, he was simply the biggest man in town. Part of my periodic growth-measuring was to see how much closer I could come to getting my arms around his fifty-five-inch waist. I don't remember if I ever made it. Little wonder that in later years his grandchildren would call him "Big Daddy"! We called him "Papa."

Papa meant working with the cattle, a drive to town sitting on his lap and pretending to help him drive the car. Papa meant meeting and entertaining new people every day, for he reveled in hospitality. Papa meant an hour or two of yarns and jokes to extend the Thanksgiving or Christmas Day meal until finally he would join us in yawning at his own stories. Above all, Papa meant the thrill of hunting deer and wild turkey in the late fall.

But Papa also meant business. More than once I learned that the fifty-five-inch belt had another function than simply holding up Papa's pants. And strangely, as I grew into my teens, I began to develop a fear of him, a fear that made it impossible for me to talk to him about the deeper things on my mind and heart. He was a very emotive man and tremendously tender at heart, but sometimes it seemed he felt the only outlet worthy of himself was his volcanic temper. I feared to cross him, and if our opinions differed, I simply did not talk about them.

It was not for his lack of goodness. On one occasion, as we were preparing to sit down to dinner, I feigned the courtesy of pulling out the chair for Aunt Margaret. I did not push it back under her, letting her almost hit the floor before I caught her. Papa's anger blazed and his right hand slapped my left cheek like the flash of a striking rattler. I was dazed and ashamed of myself. And as I toyed with my food I became more ashamed because both Aunt Margaret and Papa came to believe it was accidental. Papa apologized. That night after I went upstairs and crawled in bed, the weight of the whole event smothering me, I heard Papa's heavy footsteps on the stairs. I froze as his mighty frame blocked the faint light of the doorway. He came over to me, knelt down at the bed and repeated his apology.

"That's all right," I said.

Then he kissed me on the brow and said good-night.

For years afterwards I could not explain to myself why I did not have the courage to confess the truth.

But so much did I fear him. I was born with a foot that turned in, and even after much therapy I walked pigeon-toed. This seemed to irritate Papa, and he would use every occasion to tell me to "walk straight," even when strangers were around. When we would be working cattle in the pens on a cold winter morning, he would not allow me to put my hands in my pockets. They should be kept free, he said, in case a steer charged and I needed to reach for the fence. I couldn't see what difference the breadth of cloth made in speed, especially since it would keep my hands warm, limber, and agile. His judgment, I felt, was simple tyranny. But I didn't dare say so.

The fact is—I see it now—my father idolized me. He wanted me to become everything he was—powerful, self-disciplined, manly—and everything he could not be. And sometimes, especially as he saw me growing away from him, he wanted too hard.

Much of my later life was shaped by my image of my father, even my idea of God. Like my father, he was the

11

mighty one to be pleased, the one not to cross. But he was not the one in whose presence I could relax and pour out my soul. Much in my memory of my father would need healing. The medicine would be a mixture of the memory of my father's goodness, the discovery in myself of all the things I hated in him, and the Lord's grace.

With my mother, on the other hand, I could share my greatest excitements. She was strict; in fact, I think I got more spankings from her than from Papa. But something about her made me want to share everything that excited me. I began to write at an early age; in fact, at the age of eleven I was printing a monthly tabloid with eventually numbered some six hundred subscribers. Mama was the one with whom I could hardly wait to share everything I wrote. And it was probably because she saw not its imperfections but its promise.

My brothers were five to eight years older than I. They were close enough in age to one another to do things together—riding, working, rodeos, hunting trips. They formed a musical trio of violin, guitar, and mandolin. I was too far behind in age to keep up with them, so I had to learn how to survive on my own. Writing and publishing and the kinds of things I could do by myself were the primary outlets. I developed a great sense of independence even from my peers at school.

Those years were not without religious experience. Papa was a strict Catholic of Irish descent, and Mama was a convert. Sunday morning was always a routine of rounding up the family and driving the five miles to St. Stanislaus Church in Bandera. Though the population of the town was less than a thousand, and the Catholic population was a minority even of that, there was a Catholic grade school attached to the church, and it was staffed by the Sisters of Charity of the Incarnate Word. It was here that I began school at the age of six. I remember very little about that first year, but one scene made a deep impression on me. Standing before the class with a crucifix in her hand, Sister described the sufferings of Jesus in the passion and spoke of his great love. I was moved to the point of numbness.

Papa was so committed to giving us a religious education that the next year when my older brothers were of high-school age, he moved the whole family to San Antonio where we could be placed in Catholic schools. Adapting to city life, even for only five days a week, had its hilarious moments, but it meant that my education from then on would be a unique combination of country life, city life, and religious influence.

On New Year's Eve during my sophomore year, word came that my brother Charlie had been killed in the battle of Tarawa in the South Sea Islands. I was too young to understand fully what this loss meant, but I could see the effect it had on the rest of the family. The cultural Catholicism which had been our heritage was inadequate to cope with this experience which shattered the very heart of our family. What we needed was naked faith, and Charlie's death showed how little of that we had. Papa had lost one of the sons he had idolized, and he seemed to withdraw like Job to the dungheap to scrape his wound in bitter silence. It was as if he could not forgive the Lord for this. "If it is not he, who then is it?" (Job 9:24). The rest of us tried the alternative of forgetting, applying a local anesthetic to a portion of our memory so that we could go on living. But the wound we had suffered was not healed.

The Lord began a healing, but it was by taking another son of the family away—me. During a retreat of the next school year, I experienced a sudden crystallization of awareness that I could call conversion. I must admit there was a good deal of fear and negative father-image about the way I received the Lord into my life at that time, but as a result of the experience I began to attend Mass daily, sometimes even at the effort of getting up at five-thirty in the morning. One day, after receiving the sacrament of penance, I was kneeling in prayer and just looking at the tabernacle. Suddenly I felt a kind of tug inside me that almost took my breath away. It was a mixture of fear and delight, like the times my older brother had picked up my little frame and tossed me into the air and caught me in his arms. I can say no more except that I knew the experience was

13

from the Lord. I hardly dared to think that it might mean he was calling me to cast all else aside and follow him, but as the days passed, that is what it came to mean. In the spring I announced my intention to enter the Society of Mary.

All that Mama said was, "If that is what you want . . ." though it was with tears. Papa wanted me to wait another year, but he said he wouldn't refuse to let me go sooner. The day I was to leave on the train for St. Louis, he made some important-business excuse that required his saying good-bye at the ranch. I walked with him to the green Chevrolet pick-up. He said a few words, then shook my hand and jumped into the pick-up and gunned it in an attempt to get out of my sight before I could see him bawling like a baby. Fifteen years later, when I gave him my first priestly blessing, I could see how he had been healed even of the loss of Charlie. Somehow, in the whirlwind of his Jobian faith, he had come to see that letting go to the Lord was not to lose but to get back a hundredfold. When I anointed him on his deathbed three years later, he took my hand and moved it gently back and forth in the best embrace he could manage.

Maryhurst in Missouri was quite different from the ranch in Texas—colder weather, taller trees, soccer instead of horses, and the dark endless tunnels they called hallways in the motherhouse. It was one of the happiest years of my life. I rejoiced in newfound friends—though I still knew how to keep a bit aloof—and the lives of the saints became a passion with me. Of the many I read, the life of Teresa of Avila made the deepest impression. I was excited by these heroes and I wanted to be like them—then and there.

The next year of novitiate began a curious development in my life. I was taught that the conquest of sanctity is a science and an art, extremely intricate and organized. I'm sure I derived benefit from this organized approach, but it put me on the road of seeking perfection more as a work than as an opening to grace. It reinforced my tendency toward isolation and independence. Close friendships are dangerous things, I was told.

And so I began to view the friendships that I had enjoyed so much the year before as potentially harmful, and learned to keep a cool and distrustful distance. It was more important to excel than to enjoy putting the other first.

From then on, through the years of college formation, the experience of Paul was mine. "I advanced beyond many of my own age, so extremely zealous was I for the traditions of my fathers" (Gal. 1:14). How well the Lord was preparing me, even in my experience of those years, for understanding the Paul I would one day write books about! I was a proud little Christian bastard—and I use the term advisedly, for my *experience* of the Lord still lacked the freedom of sonship. I was out to prove to myself, to others, and to God, that I was perfect, and if I had to admit that I wasn't there yet, it should at least have been obvious that I was perfectly programmed. Sanctity was a race, and passing up others was so much assurance I would be first to the goal. Little wonder that I had trouble truly receiving others' love. They wanted to love me as I was, defects and all, but I would have none of that. I wanted to be perfect so that others would *have* to love me—they would have no choice!

As I recall the days of the seminary in Fribourg, Switzerland, where I was ordained and where I did my doctoral studies, I remember vividly a bike-hike I took through the mountains with four or five of my peers. I recall distinctly the passion I felt to lead the pack, even though one of my brothers was having trouble with his bicycle. I let someone else worry with him. To be first to the foot of the mountain and first on top—that's all that interested me. This scene is symbolic of where I was spiritually, of how important it had become for me to excel rather than to put others first. It was more important to get to the mountain first than it was to share the ride with my brothers.

It was not until a year after my ordination to the priesthood that the Lord hit me between the eyes with the inadequacy of this approach. I was making a Better World retreat in Segovia, Spain. Sitting under a big tree

15

in the open air, surrounded by retreatants, I heard the retreat master speak of those who pursue even charity as *their* charity and delight in taking daily thermometer readings on the intensity of *their* charity. I felt as if I had been hit by a two-by-four. Yes, *my* charity! What a contradiction in terms when put that way! For if there is any passion, human or divine, that does not seek its own, it is love (1 Cor. 13:5). But what a perfect picture of the contradiction I was trying to live—even under the guise of Christian holiness.

I returned to Fribourg to finish my doctorate in Saint Paul. Even as I pursued my research, I was exploring the implications of my new discovery about love. Then, after six years abroad, I returned to the States. My first assignment involved teaching at my old alma mater, Central Catholic High School in San Antonio. I was still in the theological clouds, and I still wonder how those teenagers managed to put up with this Doctor of Theology who was so impressed with the salvific power of his theological distinctions.

At the end of the next year I made a Cursillo. Sitting in the sweltering June heat, I listened to blue-collar workers from Kelly Field, some of whom had hardly finished grade school, talk about Jesus as a personal experience in their lives, what a difference Jesus made to them, and how their lives had never since been the same. Then and there I saw that the good news is fundamentally a personal experience of Jesus so powerful one is excited about it to the point of noncontainment. These men had the kind of personal Christ-wisdom I had studied about in Paul without deeply experiencing. I had begun again to see holiness in others. I felt a compelling desire to have that kind of faith, so inadequately developed in my theological head-trip of the previous years.

And yet, in the Lord's plan my theological preparation had destined me to teach theology, and I was appointed not only to teach at St. Mary's University in San Antonio but also to head up the graduate program in theology there. I was a success on both the undergraduate and the graduate level. But I still had much to learn about the ways of the Lord, and he arranged events in my life to bring about a new growth.

During the Christmas holidays of 1966-67, I managed to drive a thorn into my knee while mountain-climbing. Resisting detection by X-ray, it stayed lodged there over a year, disabling me from any serious physical recreation during that time. To amuse myself I took up the guitar. The next summer, I began to make up guitar ballads on the prophets I was teaching. The songs had a country twang which did nothing to conceal my Texas roots. I never intended them for anything more than recreation; the guitar seemed a bit incompatible with a professor's image. But there's nothing wrong with singing in your study, is there?

It did not at all occur to me that singing the message was really much closer to the prophetic experience than talking about the prophets academically, for it meant a greater commitment of my whole person to the message which the Lord obviously meant to go beyond a professor's lectern. It had been that for the prophets themselves; there is even some evidence that Ezekiel was a balladeer (Ezek. 33:32).

I discovered that my students wanted that *more* which the sung version of the prophets expressed. And so, with all kinds of feelings about the impropriety of mixing the minstrel with the scholar, I gradually yielded to the invitation to record these songs. One step led to another till there were four albums on the prophets, three in English and one in Spanish, going into Bible classrooms throughout the Western Hemisphere. To this day I don't understand why so many people bought these records, which musically are so much the work of an amateur. But I am happy that they brought light and joy to many. Paul thrice asked the Lord to remove his own "thorn in the flesh"—and I know now why it was over a year before he removed mine. God's ways are not our ways—thank God!

The time was soon to come when the desire to sing would fade. "By the streams of Babylon we sat and wept . . . On the willows there we hung up our harps . . . How can we sing a song of the Lord in a foreign

17

land?" (Ps. 137:1-4). Not long after the singing success I entered a spiritual and emotional exile, where the guitar gathered dust and my tongue stuck to the roof of my mouth. The securities which had supported me to this point in my life began to erode. For one thing, the stable church I had known began to fall apart. When Pope John and Vatican II relaxed the tight controls, the repressed adolescence of thousands created household chaos. But more than that, in my own personal life I began to feel the horrible limitations of my own strengths. My aloofness, independence, and self-sufficiency had not brought me oneness with others, and I began to painfully feel my alienation. I noticed how preoccupied I was with my self-image and reputation, how many tasks I had taken on precisely to prove (to myself, primarily) how good I was—and therefore how worthy of being loved! In the words of an advertisement I saw recently, I was feeling "the awesome responsibility of being the very best"—and it was killing me.

Not realizing the root of my trouble at first, I tried to react in the only way I knew—to seize even greater control. I was approaching the age of forty, and perhaps I was feeling the kind of middle-age depression which my cousin-doctor tells me is quite common—realizing that one's life is about to crest with most of one's life-dreams unrealized.

In the summer of 1968, still impressed with my ability to do everything, I took on the preaching of six week-long retreats, besides the regular summer session at the University. In the middle of July, after a succession of sleepless nights, I went to my doctor, who told me, "Drop everything at once. Go to the ranch and take a six week rest." The diagnosis: emotional exhaustion.

It was true. Interiorly I was wound up tighter than a tourniquet. I dreaded facing people. I just wanted to run away but there was nowhere to go, I felt, to find what I needed.

The rest and the great outdoors of my boyhood brought physical strength, but I knew the deeper root of my problem was still unhealed. I still felt like a spectator at the dance of life—not like one so involved in the dancing as to forget myself. I wasn't even sure life was a dance. The dancers, I suspected, are the phonies. But I wasn't eager to affirm that my spectator position was real either.

At about this time, a few people began to gather weekly at our scholasticate residence on St. Mary's campus to pray. I did not attend, but I heard a lot of talk about the Holy Spirit, about tongues and prophecy and such things that made me suspicious about the mental balance of the people who attended. Some of the members of my community went to the meetings, however, and I became impressed with the change I saw come over them. I saw greater love, joy, peace, and patience in them, and these I could identify as Paul's fruits of the Spirit (Gal. 5:22). I was particularly impressed with the spontaneity and even enthusiasm with which they were willing to take up the dull and monotonous chores in the community—doing the dishes, cleaning the house, serving at table—*putting others first!* I sometimes did those chores, when I felt they were expected of me, but I certainly didn't enjoy them very much.

I began to see that they had something I lacked, something I needed, something I wanted. I decided to go and find out what turned them on so much. I went to a prayer meeting.

By now the prayer group had grown to a regular attendance of fifty to sixty persons. My first feeling was great discomfort. There was an exuberance and a freedom of outward expression that was alien to my way of praying. There seemed to be a hypnotic preoccupation with praise of the Lord. This bothered me for I did not feel there was that much in my life to be praising the Lord for—Job's laments seemed to fit my experience better. And yet, precisely at this time, I had been writing a commentary on some of the Old Testament prayers and psalms in which I underscored precisely the absorption in praise, a repetitive praising of the Lord that defied rational analysis and could only be explained by the exaltation of a spirit chanting almost ecstatically.

My prayer until then had begun with bringing all my problems to the Lord, complaining about them, then rising enough to ask him to do something about them, "if you can" (Mark 9:22), but then concluding with the burden of the anxieties slumping back upon me again. This is what I now call lower-parabola prayer. The prayer I was finding so strange was just the opposite in its movement. These people began with praise, repeated and chanted almost *ad nauseam,* and then they began witnessing to the fantastic things the Lord was doing in their lives, and this led to even greater intensity of praise. It was as if the praises sent up were seeding the clouds, and then came a flood of wonders, with more praises resulting. It certainly was different. It's what I call upper-parabola prayer. My "lower-parabola" trajectory of prayer had collided with their "upper-parabola"—and it was unsettling.

I knew I secretly wanted what I saw, but I was scared to death at the price that might be asked. Here I sat in intellectual control (or so I viewed myself) of all my experience, even of my experience of the Lord. I must check out at the gate of rationality whatever I experience. That, after all, is what a theologian, a professor, a wise and respected scholar is supposed to do. The only problem—which I hated like hell to admit—was that I was having less and less life-giving experience to check out! I began to perceive that the chief experience I was really having was precisely the increasingly frustrating passion to "check out" everything and everyone, yes, I must admit it now, even the Lord.

Some power was moving the prayer meeting, and it was converting people, changing them, healing them. Some spoke of conversion from lives of great sin— alcoholism, sex, drugs. My ministerial eagerness first responded, "This charismatic stuff looks like the best missionary technique I've seen yet." And then I began in some way to feel the Lord looking at me—spectator, bystander, judge. Here Jesus was banqueting with Levi and Zacchaeus and Magdalene and asking me where I stood. I could not help but feel myself among the Pharisees standing outside the door and trying to check all of this out through my academic categories. And then I realized that it was not sinners that Jesus failed with; it was the "good" people whose "goodness" was so sufficient they could not hear the good news of the better life to which Jesus called them. So it had become with me. My Christianity had become professionalism, and behind that professionalism was not the sinner or even the little child of the Gospels. It was the self-righteous Pharisee.

I could hardly suspect, in the nervous sweat of my discomfort at the prayer meeting, that there was already a stream of life deep within me waiting to be tapped. The release of it would amply compensate for the pain of crushing the rock holding it back. I little realized the force of that river, for I had kept it well covered over for years with layers of protective stone. It was an old river, in a sense, for it had been there in some way since my youth. I would later call it the gift of the Holy Spirit. What I did not realize was how much the release of that gift would mean the release of pent-up energies within me that would utterly stupefy me with their power. What frightened me for the moment, I suppose, was the realization that all my defensive reaction, "But I've had the Holy Spirit since my baptism!" however theologically exact, also covered over the fact that though *I* may have had the Holy Spirit, *he* was far from having *me*. The crazy "baptism of the Holy Spirit" of which the charismatics spoke, and of which the outward gesture would be nothing more than kneeling and asking to be prayed over, might be just the thing I needed—and feared—the most: the gift of *being given* to the Lord in a new way, a way in which I would let *him* take over the controls.

Whatever moved me, I don't know, but on Christmas Eve, 1970, I stepped forward and asked to be prayed over. Some of the people who prayed over me I admired greatly, but some were persons whose psychological stability I questioned. To accept their prayer as efficacious for me was another way of losing control. Jesus never promised he would channel his life to men through a perfect church. But to experience the life he offers, I must not despise the channel he chooses.

I did not know exactly what I was asking for. I asked for an infilling of the Holy Spirit. I did not ask for specific gifts, and especially do I remember not asking for tongues. I didn't know what tongues meant (I still had to understand!), and after all, it was the least of the gifts. If the Lord wanted to give it to me, fine, but I felt sure I really didn't need it, and I would just as soon he give it to somebody who did!

As I knelt there, hearing the voices of those praying over me, many of them babbling in tongues, I felt a warmth and a tapping entry into the rock within me. I began to feel a bubbling inside—yes, that is the best image I have for it, a bubbling. It was just there and I didn't know what to do with it.

One of the ways in which I sought to release it was by finishing the last three chapters of a book I was writing—and I did it in less than three days. But the bubbling was still there. On New Year's Day, as I drove to the ranch to visit my family, I felt moved just to relax and let the bubbling come out however it would. It came out in a melody without words. Three days later words came to fit the melody: "The Spirit of the Lord has touched my soul . . ." (Little did I suspect that a new album had begun then and there.) The melody came to me on New Year's Day, the words on the feast of the Epiphany of our Lord—but the bubbling from which it flowed was the Lord's Christmas gift to me a week before.

Far from being spent by the song, the bubbling was still there. It seemed to go beyond what I could put in either melody or words. Could this be the gift of tongues? O Lord, please not that! I then spoke with one of my own theology students—a man I had trained in the Scriptures!—about his experience with tongues. I became more attracted, though still afraid. I began to study the New Testament passages with a passion and an interest I had never had before. I concluded that tongues was not an experience of being zapped suddenly with a new language spoken somewhere on the face of the earth (at least not directly), and that unless I actually moved my lips and started babbling praise nothing would happen. The gift, then, was the courage to be that foolish for the Lord—and that free. To the last resistance of my pride, the Lord seemed to say, "Will you have the humility to ask for the least of the gifts? Will you step forth and let go, trusting that I will carry you?"

I was still afraid to let go in the presence of my former student. Frankly, the whole prospect frightened me to death. What would it do to my professional image?

I went to my room, closed my door, knelt down— and let go. I stopped a couple of times as if looking at myself in the mirror, and reflected how stupid this sounded. But then I tried to ignore that, realizing I felt the same way when I first tried to dance. I began to focus on the Lord, and then it was easier to let go. More and more came. I was singing God knows what, but I felt the awkward yet liberating freedom of not having to know or care what syllable or note would come next. And then I began to feel, for the first time in my life perhaps, like the buzzards I had as a child watched gliding in the sky for hours without flapping their wings— they let the wind carry them. (Sorry about mentioning *buzzard* when you were expecting something more esthetic like dove or seagull, but I'm from Texas, and it's the *wind,* not the bird, that gets the credit. In Texas the most repulsive bird is the most graceful flier—and it's all because he lets the wind do the work!)

So that's tongues! Praising God by letting the Spirit do it in you, for you, with you! And not caring what syllable or tone comes next! All right, Lord, but not in public, please!

The Lord had his hour for that, too. I was invited to celebrate an afternoon Mass at the convent of the Sisters of Divine Providence in Castroville for some kind of regional meeting being held there. They sang my new Spirit song at the end of Mass. Sister Charlene invited me to stay for supper, and then for a prayer meeting. Contrary to my plans, I accepted. During the prayer meeting one of the young sisters said she had been very burdened and would like to be prayed over. Naturally, with my compulsion to preside, I was one of the first to step forward to pray over her. Nice, rational prayers (I was very practiced in that kind of praying), and then a dead silence fell over all, a moment of intensely quiet prayer. I felt a nudge that said, "Now."

I said, "Lord, you're kidding!"

"Now!"

"But this is stupid!"

"Now!"

I plunged and began to sing in tongues. Several others, to my amazement, joined in—and the spirit of the whole prayer meeting seemed to be lifted like a jet plane climbing above the clouds.

That night I drove home singing the Lord's praise at the top of my voice. I am surprised I was not stopped by a patrol car for driving while intoxicated. I don't know what answer I would have given, other than telling the patrolman, "That's what they thought on Pentecost morning, too!"

My life since then has been so different, so rich, so full of inexplicable events that I cannot begin to relate them. I have come to realize that the gifts of the Spirit are not toys but tools—made for the building of the kingdom. On one occasion, a nun of Indian descent, whose father had been murdered on the reservation precisely because he had tried to help a delinquent boy, came to me to ask for prayers. After praying over her for a few minutes I began to sing in tongues. When I had finished, she stood up with tears in her eyes. "I have, in faith, experienced the resurrection of my father. And some of your words I recognized as words of the Sioux dialect my grandmother used to speak." I had nothing to do with that, except to surrender to the Lord as best I could while praying.

I have witnessed physical healing—like that of Gus whose hearing, lost for twenty-five years, came back completely when the community of believers at Biscayne College in Miami asked the Lord for it.

Most of all, I have witnessed the powerful inner healings of soul and spirit—the healing of marriages and families, the healing of long-festering hatreds. And to me the rebirth of love and forgiveness is the surest sign that this is the Lord's work.

My greatest witness to the Lord's deep healing is myself. I have found a new strength and vitality, a greater willingness to risk for the Lord, a greater ability to cope with stress and chaos. Many of my early painful memories have been healed, and I have been able to say "praise God" for the whole of my own past, that of which I have written and that which remains unsaid. The Lord has put the dispersed energies together more and more too. Especially has he helped me to accept my uniqueness with its grandeur and its limitations and shown me how to love even myself, with less and less need for the kinds of reassurance I used to seek.

The reality of my healing is matched only by the realization of how far I have yet to go. The Lord has at least given me to see that life is not a race to be first to the mountain but a daily yielding to his Spirit, wherever and however he leads. It is not a question of beating my wings but of learning how to lend them to the Wind.

In the chapters that follow I offer some personal reflections on the life in the Spirit. These meditations will be a mixture of Biblical reflections and personal experience, sometimes more of one than the other. May I suggest that before you read each chapter, you pause to pray, asking that the Lord speak to you as you read. For I would much rather he tell you what *you* need to hear than that you remember anything I have written.

CHAPTER TWO

Body, Soul, and Spirit

May God himself, the author of peace, make you holy through and through, and may your whole being, *spirit, soul, and body,* be kept blameless for the coming of our Lord Jesus Christ." This final prayer from Paul's first letter to the Thessalonians (5:23) is more than a liturgical finale. It speaks to me and to every Christian of the makeup of the whole self. I am a three-dimensional being, it tells me, and I understand myself as a whole only when, looking toward the Lord's coming, I allow his sanctifying power to touch every bit of me, and that means body, soul, and spirit.

I am not accustomed to think of myself in this way. I once learned to view myself as body and soul, and that was all. Aristotle, reshaping some of the categories of his master Plato, said that man is composed of body, soul (by which he simply meant the principle of man's animal life), and mind (*nous*). Paul, who built, as we shall see, on the biblical view of man as given in Genesis 2:7, tells me that I am a trinity within myself, but not after the fashion of Aristotle. I am body, soul, and spirit. What does this mean for me?

BODY

I am body. The Greek word is *soma.* If I listen to the philosophers of old, who heavily influenced the West, I experience my body primarily as a limitation. Bodiliness or materiality, they say, limits form or perfection. Because I am body I am just this and not something else at the same time. It accounts for my uniqueness, but it also by the very same token separates me from the rest of the material world and of course from other human beings. I cannot occupy the same space with another body, any more than two automobile bodies can occupy the same spot, as every collision amply demonstrates. Every time I've been squeezed out of an elevator I have realized that someone's bodiliness has conflicted with my own, and his won out. As I see the elevator taking off without me, I conclude that Plato and Aristotle were right. Bodiliness really limits me. It's a barrier.

But there are times when I rejoice that I am body. When I shake the hand of a friend or embrace someone I love, I am glad we both have hands and arms. Then I know that the Greeks didn't have the whole truth about me, for my body can be a bridge.

It is in fact this latter view that I learn most clearly from the Bible. I am *Adam* from the *adamah;* my most basic name is Earthman because from the earth I have been taken (Gen. 2:4). I shall never lose my brotherhood with all that is lumpy, solid, space-taking, and collision-prone. All that is a part of me, and I am a part of all of that. If this lot causes the Job in me to scream, it also causes the Francis in me to sing of the sun and moon, the animals and the birds as my brothers and sisters. Whether I am an evolutionist or not, I must basically accept the insight of Teilhard de Chardin that I am the fifty-seventh cousin of the bread-mold. Wherever my head may be, my feet are rooted like a tree on the earth and my first community is with all created things.

It may not be surprising, then, for me to learn that redemption means the returning of all creation to God through my *body* (Rom. 8:19-23), and that when the body experiences the fullness of redemption, it will bring brother universe with it (cf. Eph. 1:21-23; Phil. 3:-21).

Nor should it surprise me to discover that when Paul looks for an image to express the intense unity to which all men are called in Christ, he finds no better image than that of *body*. Because the risen Christ is body and I am body, I can be one with him in a way that is mysteriously organic (1 Cor. 6:14, 15, 20; 12:13; Eph. 5:-

30), and in the same mystery I can be organically united with all others joined to him (Eph. 4:25).

The Greek tells me that my body is the tomb for my soul: *soma sema*. That sounds nice but it could hardly lead to the kind of challenge of Hebrews 13:3: "Remember those who are in prison, as though in prison with them; and those who are ill-treated, *since you are also in the body*." "Since you are also in the *body*" in the parallel structure is simply a way of saying, "as though you were being ill-treated with them." The body relates me to the suffering of others as my own. Bodiliness is not a cause of separation but of solidarity. Whatever happens to my brothers in the flesh happens to me. Their rejoicing is my rejoicing; their mourning is my mourning.

Body is so radical and intimate to what I am that it sometimes means just *me* (Rom. 12:1; Phil. 1:20; Eph. 5:28). And to be saved is not to jettison the body but to redeem it (Rom. 8:23). So the Word of God promises me not escape from bodiliness but the resurrection of it.

To be fully Christian then I must accept my bodiliness and the brotherhood it gives me with the universe, with other men, and with my fellow-members of the Body of Christ.

SOUL

I am soul, *psyche*. This means many things, and first of all that I am living: "Man became a *living psyche*" says the Greek Bible in Genesis 2:7. But I am living in a way that the rock or the rose or the dog never dreamed of. The rock and the rose can never see themselves being rock and rose. The dog's only chance of seeing himself is to go to the pond. But I can see myself by just deciding to do so. I can contain myself in myself. I can be a context for myself. I can be my own mirror.

One spring afternoon on a walk with one of my brothers, I leaned over and plucked a bluebonnet. "Tim," I said, "look. It really looks like a bonnet, doesn't it? No wonder they made it the state flower of

Texas. But it has no idea that it is beautiful. It can't blush. It doesn't even know that it's a bluebonnet. Only you and I do. We give the bluebonnet intelligence. We give it reflection." Trite and obvious. As trite and obvious as the millionth bluebonnet of the millionth spring, that needs me to say, "Wow!"

Soul is my ordination to lordship. It is my title to superiority over all the creation of which I am brother through *soma*. I am to *name* things (Gen. 2:19f.). And that means first of all that I can grasp and understand them, or at least that I have a right to. As man, I have been made master of the universe: "You have set him over the works of your hands, you have put all things under his feet" (Ps. 8:6). Even when I can't exert physical control, I can understand, and that is to control. The mountain may be falling upon me and killing me; but at least I know it is a mountain and I know that I am dying. Nothing else does.

Thus, although Paul does not mention the mind, *nous,* in this triple line-up, it can hardly be far from his thought, for the rational activity of the mind, especially when it is considered independently of faith and the Spirit, is what constitutes for Paul the *psychic* man, the "natural" man (1 Cor. 2:14). This means that the soul and the mind have their limits. Science is the great achievement of this psychic man. It has served me well in many ways—when it has not exceeded its limits. When it has tried to be the total explanation of my existence, it has become tyranny. Western man has experienced reason both as blessing and as curse. The Enlightenment proclaimed Reason as Messiah and even enthroned her on a cathedral altar. She brought us the computer—and triggered the primal scream that we were being depersonalized. She took us into the outer space of the heavenly bodies only to make us more conscious of how vast is the inner space between us in our own earthly bodies even when we live in the same neighborhood, yes, even in the same house. She gave us wonder drugs only to provide those dying of spiritual hunger an easy means to choose suicide by degrees, drug addiction. Man's body may live by bread and his mind by knowledge. But man the person lives neither by bread alone nor by knowledge alone. There must be something more. For man the person is also spirit; and until his spirit meets spirit, man is not fully man. As water becomes all that water is meant to be when it offers drink to man and thus shares in man's life, so man becomes all that man is meant to be when he meets God in the spirit.

SPIRIT

I am spirit. "The Lord God formed man out of the clay of the ground and blew into his nostrils the *breath* of life, and so man became a living being" (Gen. 2:7). What makes the clay in me really live, what makes my body and soul find their full meaning, is that the breath of life has been given me by the Lord. The Greek word most often used to render *breath* or *spirit* is *pneuma*. It is God's most direct gift and that which makes me most like him. It is another way of saying that God created me in his own image, after his own likeness (Gen. 1:26f). Unlike the animals, with whom I share animated life, I am most God-like because the pneuma, the spirit or breath of the Lord, has entered me.

What is this *spirit?* On the crudest level, it is breath, as intimate to me as life itself. It suggests however that there is a more inward breath by which I take in the air of the divine world. If *psyche* is the inward principle of life which animates me, *pneuma* is my self as born from above and facing upward, my openness to self-transcendence, to movement beyond where I now stand. This is suggested by the very fact that the literal definition of pneuma is *wind* or *breathing,* and its very meaning is therefore movement. It is my capacity to be moved by the power of God.

Not that the endowment with spirit means that I automatically encounter God in his intimate personhood. Spirit is rather an anonymous orientation toward the source of life, whatever or whoever that is considered to be. Those who yield to the tendency of the spirit and live by it are perhaps not too different from those whom John classifies as being "of the light" (John 3:-16-21) or "of the truth" (John 18:37) or those whom Paul describes as accepting the love of the truth, the love of the dawn though they see not yet the day, the orientation of their whole being toward the light though they have not yet encountered it in the person and message of Jesus Christ (2 Thess. 2:10). Augustine would probably be very comfortable with this description for his "church of the pagans," those whose hearts are restless till they rest in God.

Pneuma, then, is my operation outreach. It is not inner grasp—that is the work of the *psyche* and the *nous*, the soul and the mind. *Pneuma* is rather the thrust to stretch beyond what I have already attained. It is the reach beyond the grasp, of which Browning wrote: "Man's reach must exceed his grasp, or what's a heaven for?"

This capacity is contacted and engaged when God reveals himself to me in his Son. To become a Christian is, according to Paul, not simply to say the yes of faith to the word of God; it is also a yielding of spirit to Spirit. "Our gospel came to you not only in word but also in power and in the Holy Spirit" (1 Thess. 1:5). And Paul asks the Galatians who are thinking of returning to Law as the source of their life whether it was the law or faith that brought them the experience of the Spirit (Gal. 3:2, 5). As the child just born from its mother's womb must now begin to breathe the air of the new world into which he is born, so must the child of God begin to breathe with the breath of the Spirit (John 3:5-8).

Paul is very clear on the matter. He speaks of the Holy Spirit bearing united witness with our spirit that we are God's sons (Rom. 8:16). What does this mean? The *witness* of which he speaks means *testimony,* or totally convincing evidence of the kind that a lawyer looks for to support his case. Now the claim in this case is that we are the sons of God; proof that this is not an empty word is the Holy Spirit who bears united witness with our spirit—that is, he makes us *experience* the sonship given.

The experience of sonship is the experience of a relationship, and that means the interaction of two related beings. On the one hand it means to know God as Father: "The proof that you are sons is the fact that God has sent forth into our hearts the spirit of his Son who cries out 'Abba! Father!'" (Gal. 4:6, Rom. 8:15). God is no longer known in the darkness as a mighty impersonal force, first cause, the threatening stick—or whatever other half-baked image we might have of him. The groping of the spirit to know who he is has ended in a mighty exclamation, "Father!" or better, since the Aramaic *Abba* is really the form of endearment, "Daddy!" And the statement is not just a statement. The Spirit makes us *cry out*. (And the Greek *kradzon* even sounds like it.)

I can never read that verse without recalling an incident that happened on my family's ranch a few years ago. My eight-year-old namesake-nephew George went down to the lake to fish. After patient waiting for the line to wiggle, he hauled in a large bass that later weighed out to be eight-and-a-half pounds.

Landing the monster nearly wore him out, but he was so excited he ran to the nearby lounge and picked up the extension phone to call his father about it. His father already happened to be on the phone on an important business call. This didn't daunt little George. He burst in, "Daddy! Daddy! Daddy!" So great was his excitement that his father thought something terrible had happened, perhaps a drowning. "What is it, George?" he asked.

"Daddy! I just caught a thirty-pound fish!"

Aside from the fact that little George showed that he was on his way to being a good fisherman, by the exaggeration as well as by the fact, the excitement of the cry, "Daddy!" illustrates precisely what Paul is trying to convey about the effect of the Spirit upon us. The Spirit, connecting with our Spirit, makes us cry with excitement: "Abba!" The cry is, of course, more than simply the sharing of an exciting surprise in our life. The surprise is precisely the recognition of God as Father.

So the Spirit personalizes God for us. He also, of course, makes us cry out, "Jesus is Lord!", for it is only by the Holy Spirit that we can say that (1 Cor. 12:3). And so, he personalizes Jesus for us too: Jesus is no longer a statistic or a history-book figure, he is a personal friend whom it is exciting to know.

But the Spirit also personalizes us to ourselves, and this is the other pole of the relationship. Humanly speaking, we discover our identity primarily in our relationships. As we grow through childhood and adolescence into maturity, we gather, hopefully from the affirming response of parents, family, and friends, that we are somebody, that we are worthwhile, and that our name stands for something. Part of this coming-to-awareness and self-assurance comes from our accomplishments; but it comes more deeply from the awareness that we are loved and that we mean something to someone. The experience of the Holy Spirit builds on this, and, as the Spirit is wont to do, transcends it. The Spirit is God's love poured into my heart (Rom. 5:5), and it tells me who I am in relation to the very source and goal of my being: I am God's child, his beloved one.

This is no small miracle. How few Christians really experience their sonship as more than a title! How few Christians ever have the thrilling experience with God that they might have the first time they hear from another person the words, "I love you!" But that is precisely what the Holy Spirit is all about. He is the kiss of God upon each person, consecrating that person's uniqueness.

This insight has been well grasped by the Eastern church in its rich iconography. There are ikons of Christ, the king and almighty, ikons of God the Father, ikons of the Virgin and Child, ikons of the saints. But there is no ikon of the Holy Spirit. Why? Because each person who is touched by the Spirit becomes himself an ikon of the Holy Spirit. The Holy Spirit has no face of his own—he is what happens when the Son faces the Father and the Father faces the Son. And he is what happens to make us face the Father and the Father face us.

The point here is that all this is possible for me because I am spirit. The ancient Egyptians said man is made up of body, soul, and *name*. They were not too far from the Pauline view, because the full consummation of the spirit means discovering my own name in discovering God's. Whenever I cry out "Abba" I am also crying out who I am, all my own lovable uniqueness as his son.

BALANCE AND INTERACTION
OF BODY, SOUL, AND SPIRIT

Body, soul, and spirit are not three compartments but rather three different modes in which I exist, three different ways of understanding myself and my relatedness.[1] I am complete and whole, the Bible tells me,

---

[1] For those of my readers who have been formed in dualistic, body-soul categories, and for those who use the term *psyche,* as the psychologists do, as the base of many functions, I offer the following suggestions. The three biblical terms are less functional and more relational in their meanings. Thus the biblical "body" connotes much more than simply the material element of the person's constitution; it stresses relationship with the cosmos and all mankind. As for soul and spirit, they too stress relationships. Aquinas sees one of the soul's capacities to be its openness to the infinite, and later Thomists speak of the soul's ability to be lifted to the divine sphere as its "obediential potency." Even Aristotle granted that the *nous* or mind had a contemplative function. Thus, if we have to make three biblical terms fit a Procrustean bed of body-soul dualism, I would say that *pneuma* is this higher function of the *psyche.* It would correspond to the religious and transcendental function of the *psyche* so important to Jung, for whom the soul "has the dignity of a creature endowed with, and conscious of, a relationship to Deity. The soul must contain in itself the faculty of relation to God" (*Psychology and Alchemy, Collected Works,* XII, 1967, p. 10). The problem I find in seeing *pneuma* as merely a function of the *psyche* is that it so overloads the category of *psyche* as to obscure the primacy of the person's pneumatic orientation. In speaking of three elements instead of two, Paul safeguards, it seems to me,

only when I have an integrated balance of body, soul, and spirit. When I try to exclude one of these elements or give one of them the place the other is made for, I become like a three-legged stool trying to stand on one or two legs—or, if on three of unequal length, I am simply not balanced.

It is, of course, possible to so emphasize the pneumatic that all reason and all human solidarity is laid aside. Such a disincarnated excess is not Christian. It is fanaticism. But we are more likely prone to neglect the *pneuma* in favor of the mind and body. This is sickness. And when it goes to the point of seeking from the *psyche* or the *soma* what only the *pneuma* can give, it approaches the demonic.

Persons who rely on brute physical strength to secure their position in life not only don't know what they are missing, they also cause pain and suffering to others. When drugs, sex, or drink become the resources to which one turns for "meaning" in life, one is really seeking to wrench the pneumatic from the somatic. It is a perversion and it doesn't work.

The psychic too can become a perversion if one seeks from it what only the *pneuma* can give. The genius who is only genius, the man of an "idea" or a "program" who pursues it to the disregard of personhood—whether it be the isolated genuis of a recluse or the tyrannical lunacy of a Hitler—is guilty of the kind of hubris described in the first pages of the Bible, an attempt to gain "knowledge" via a demonic short-cut. And the fruits now, as then, are not the tree of knowledge but the nakedness, alienation, fraternal bloodshed, and babbling disintegration which are mankind's self-chosen curse. *Psyche* and *nous* without *pneuma* cannot yield the fruits of *pneuma*.

How, positively, are body, soul, and spirit to interact?

We have long been aware of the empirical fact that body and soul interact. I was expecting an A in a course

the proper orientation of each. *Pneuma* then appears not as a mere option of transcendence but as the most crucial source of life for man fully alive.

and I got an F instead. Result: I'm so upset I can't eat my dinner or sleep that night. Or I dislike someone intensely and I get headaches when he's around. Or, inversely, the person next door lets his stereo blare into the night and keeps me awake. The next day I get depressed for lack of sleep. Medical science in recent years has had much to say about the interaction of mind and body. Well over half the diseases of mankind are classified as psychosomatic—and some authorities are willing to go as high in their estimates as eighty or ninety percent. The symptoms are somatic but the cause is psychological. The need to feel "pilled" is so great and invincible in some patients that the doctor will prescribe a *placebo,* a sugar-coated nothing that does neither harm nor good but satisfies the patient's need to need medicine. The power of the psychosomatic is indeed an empirical fact.

But let us assume now that I am also *pneuma.* If the *psyche* has such an influence on the body, might not the spirit in turn have a powerful influence on the *psyche* and through the *psyche* on the body as well? If we can speak of psychosomatic diseases, might we not also speak of pneumapsychosomatic diseases? Such diseases have psychic and somatic effects but their roots are really in the undeveloped or constricted *pneuma.*

My own experience, both personal and pastoral, has convinced me both that these diseases are an everyday occurrence and that many psychic and organic healings can be accomplished simply through the healing of the *pneuma.* Biblically speaking, the health of the *pneuma* can be judged by the energy of one's faith, the tenacity of one's hope, and the power of one's love (1 Thess. 1:3).

Often in counseling, after all the psychological analysis is done, it becomes evident that there remains the step the counselee, and only the counselee, must take if he is to experience new life. He needs very simply to get out of the boat and to start walking on the waters. But how often the counselee sees this not as life but as death itself; or, even if he sees it as the way to life, he feels powerless to do anything to budge. He is paralyzed. He lacks faith. And the absence of this strength in the pneuma has obvious psychic and often even physical effects—distress, frustration, loneliness, psychosomatic colds. It is here that faith can truly save the person. True, at this point it may be quite mixed with human faith, the risk of entrusting oneself to another person or to a community, a willingness to become vulnerable again. But precisely at this point Jesus is available. He offers what human support cannot guarantee: divine fidelity that was willing to die on a cross for those to whom he had sworn to be faithful.

Or the problem may be lack of hope—an unwillingness to dream how much better things could be; it's safer to trim the wings than to risk soaring too high. Why attempt to fly a kite this season, when so many have crashed into a tree before? But when man ceases to dream he also dies by inches. Victor Frankl observed in the concentration camps that some men died long before they should have precisely because they knew not how to hope, and others outlasted incredible counterforces because they had a hope to live by.

But the worst of these illnesses is the refusal to love. "As long as I declared not my sins, my body wasted away . . . my strength was dried up as by the heat of summer" (Ps. 32:3-4). I remember a woman who came to talk to me once during a retreat. It was near noon on a Good Friday. She had not been able to sleep for several nights, she felt that she was developing an ulcer, and she was at the point of great depression. The cause? Two persons she had to live with, she said. She was angry with them for some of the things they had done to her.

"Is this the first time you ever felt this way toward anyone?"

"Well, at home—but that was years ago."

"But you still remember, don't you? Would you like to talk about that?"

It had been her mother. She could not forgive her mother—in fact, had never really forgiven her—for the rejection she experienced in childhood.

"And is the clenched fist you're now using the one you first clenched at your mother?"

Tears came to her eyes. "Yes, I guess I never unclenched that fist all these years."

"And whoever came along looking like Mother got the same fist, too?"

It became clear that for her to be healed she would have to let go of that fist. She would have to forgive.

"But that's—that's like dying."

"Like dying on a cross, as a matter of fact. For that's when he said, 'Father, forgive them . . .'"

"But I don't know if I can do it."

"Alone you probably can't. But look at him and see if you still say you can't."

At my suggestion she opened her hands (she was too physically weak to kneel) and called into the room, as realistically as she could, her mother and the other two persons. Then she said, with the kind of pain that seemed as if she were extracting a deeply imbedded and festered thorn, "Mother, in the name of Jesus I forgive you." And then she did the same for the other two. I prayed for the infilling of the Holy Spirit. She left and went out on the hill behind the retreat house, where she threw herself on the ground and poured out her soul, groaning for an hour. At the end she breathed, "Abba—Alleluia." The hill of Good Friday had become the mount of the transfiguration of Easter morning. That night, for the first time in weeks, she slept soundly, with no knots in her stomach. By her forgiveness she had removed the obstacle to health of spirit, soul, and body.

God's love is like sunshine. It will light up not only our spirit but our mind and body as well. It is constantly available but if we block it out by excluding anyone from our love, we should not complain (and certainly we can't blame the Lord) if we soon begin to feel the effects mentally and physically. My experience has convinced me that *some* colds are "hatred" colds—bodily signs that we need to get something straightened out in our pneuma with the Lord or with a brother or sister. Our intimate makeup of body-soul-spirit is that real.

To be truly human, then, and truly alive, I must accept myself as body, soul, and spirit. And if I exclude any one of these, I am denying my very God-given nature. My body roots me like a tree in this earth and binds me to every man and every woman in the world. My soul and my mind ordain me to putting order into this world, to rising above it as the tree rises above the earth. And because I am spirit I reach out to touch heaven. For I stand with my feet firmly planted on the earth and my arms lifted toward heaven, that heaven which I can practically touch with the tips of my fingers without being able yet to grasp. But just as the tension between rootedness in the earth and stretching toward the sun is what makes the tree grow, so will it be with me in stretching from my lowly bodily roots to my infinite spiritual outreach.

CHAPTER THREE

The Language of the Christian

I am body, soul, and spirit. These dimensions of my person are not static. Rather they are like faculties that must be used if I am to grow. Each of them has a mode of operation, a language. As I learn to use that language, I begin to grow.

Creature of the earth that I am, I understand body-language more readily than any other. As a baby I did not understand the words my mother spoke to me, but her tenderness, her caresses, and her smile spoke volumes. They told me that I was good and lovable, that I was wanted, that I was worth making great sacrifices for. And even as I began to learn what certain words meant when spoken by those around me, I continued to read more in their facial expressions and bodily reactions than I did in the words they said. Now that I am an adult and have learned the sophisticated language, I still know that I cannot jettison my body or bodily experience if I am going to be real.

If God is spirit, as even my pre-Christian mind would lead me to suspect, there seems to be a real problem here. For how can what is bodily encounter what is spirit? Or, if spirit is only part of me, and I encounter God in the spirit, then how can my whole person be involved? We Christians have often despised those religions that believe heaven will consist of a round of sensual pleasures. Surely, the kingdom of God does not consist in eating and drinking, but we should be cautious about hastily dismissing the body, lest we live in some sort of spiritual illusion. Before we enter the rarefied mystery of spirit-language or even of mind language, we might best explore the mystery of body language. Mystery, yes, precisely because it is so close to us and yet it is the glorious gateway to the Spirit.

BODY LANGUAGE

Only on the assumption that we learn first from body language does the whole Jesus-phenomenon make any sense. "What we have heard, what we have seen with our eyes, what we have looked upon and our hands have touched—the Word of life—we announce to you" (1 John 1:1-3); "In him dwells the fullness of the Godhead *bodily*" (Col. 2:9). He was truly a man. He had feet that could get dirty as he walked the dust of the earth, hands that could touch—and be touched to the point of being held motionless against a cross by earth-made nails. He had a native village, and its name was Nazareth. He had a name and it was Jesus.

If he lived 2,000 years ago, does the bodily distance that separates us make it impossible for me to encounter him? There were people whom he touched, and people who touched him without ever knowing who he was. So just being able to put myself in a time machine and walk with him through Galilee would be no guarantee that I would really know him. Something more is needed, and that is faith. And yet without his touching me somehow through what I see or hear or feel I would have no platform from which to leap into that act of faith which alone lets me know him as he is. Fortunately, he anticipated this need of mine, for he promised not to leave his disciples orphans (John 14:18). He has left me with many signs of his presence, signs that invite me to move from what I have experienced with my bodily senses into the deeper faith-union with him.

The first of these signs is the living community of his disciples. Paul describes this community precisely as the *body* of the risen Christ, and if I take this seriously, as Paul did, I know that it is the Lord's plan that I should receive the Spirit in and through this body: "In one Spirit we were all baptized into one body and we were all given to drink of the same Spirit" (1 Cor 12:13). This body, we are told elsewhere, he has endowed with all kinds of gifts and services so that the body might build itself up in his life and love: "It was he who gave some men as apostles, others as prophets, others as evangelists, still others as shepherds and teachers, in order to organize the saints for active ministry in building up the body of Christ . . . for from him the whole body, growing more and more compact and closely knit together through every life-feeding contact (according to the measured activity each single part deploys), the whole body, I say, works out its increase for the building up of itself in love" (Eph. 4:11-16). It is the community that speaks to me the kind of body language that Jesus left it to speak. Through the ministry of his body, the Lord Jesus touches me with water and the word in baptism. In the bread and wine of the Eucharist, he feeds me with his own flesh and blood. Through the touch of a hand, he lays his hand upon me and anoints me for witnessing and ministry. If I marry, he ministers to me even in the touch and the word of the other who says yes. Through the sacrament of penance, he pronounces his forgiveness over my chaotic sinfulness. And, finally, in the touch of oil and the cross when I am ill, Jesus touches me to bring me health of body, mind, and spirit. Beyond these individual signs, the community of believers is itself a constant, ongoing sign for me. For in it I am constantly fed the word and the life of Jesus, constantly challenged to step out more in faith, constantly encouraged to believe in the power of the risen Lord who beckons to me through and beyond these signs.

For indeed it is not just the community that I encounter, but through it the Lord himself. For it is not just signs, even his own, that the Lord Jesus would have me believe. He would have me believe *him*. He would have me confess from my heart and with my lips "Jesus is Lord," and thus touch the very mystery of his being. Jesus' bodiliness and his church's signs do not excuse me from faith, but they invite it, and once it is given, they become one of the languages of faith, for faith in Jesus speaks a bodily language.

So, if I would grow in the Lord, I need to learn to

speak the full spectrum of this body language. In particular, I want to be part of this community's coming together to celebrate—to pray together, to hear the word together, and especially to break the Lord's bread together. Knowing that my body can pray as much as my mind and spirit do, I will realize that to kneel or to lift up my hands, to clap, to sing, to walk together in procession, even to sway and dance on occasion, is not unworthy of the Lord who takes all these bodily expressions to himself in his own bodiliness. Jesus is not an angel, and neither are his people.

Far from it. I may not particularly like those whom he has called to be my fellow disciples. I may not find the shepherd he has given me particularly stimulating. But I know that too is part of the scandal of the Good News which Jesus brought into the world—namely, that he chose fishermen, tax collectors, and sinners as his earliest disciples. He did not hesitate to share his table with them, and from their number he chose the leaders of his community. Part of my bodiliness as a Christian is to accept not only the Lord but those whom the Lord has called to share the bodily life with him and with me, and even to allow them to minister to me. "I have not come to call the righteous but sinners" (Mark 2:17).

At times I feel the bodily weight of this community. It seems to move so slowly. While the Spirit is available to give wings to anyone who asks, most of the community seems content with pedestrian pace. They do not even feel the need to ask for anything better. At times I have felt the tug to abandon the dinosaur in search of the eagle.

But then I ask what Jesus did when he felt the weight of disbelief and even rejection by his own people. The day when it became crystal clear to him that if he continued to seek out and serve his own people it would lead to his death on a cross, he had to decide whether he should continue a work he knew was doomed to human failure, or whether he should take a few steps across the border to Gentiles awaiting him with open arms and ready faith. The few encounters he had with Gentiles in his own ministry up to that point, made it

...hat instant success awaited him just across the ...r.

But he chose to stay. "Having loved his own . . . he loved them to the end" (John 13:1). Why this insanity? Because it was more important to Jesus to love than to succeed. His mission at its deepest was to reveal the kind of love God is. A love faithful to the insane degree of dying uselessly for those he loves. The day his disciples would carry the news of this love to the Gentiles, they could say, "Look at the kind of love God offers you. What he did for his own people, he would do for you. His is a love you can count on. His covenant love faithful to death is what he offers you."

I know I belong to two communities. One of them, visible and close to the point of body odor at times, is my covenant community. For me, this is my religious community, the persons with whom I have agreed to cast my lot for life. For married persons it would be the community established by the covenant of marriage. The other kind of community, less structured and more occasional, is made up of all the persons whom I find affectively satisfying, people who "turn me on," people whom I find sources of life for me. These two communities are partially congruent—some of the persons who turn me on most are members of my covenant community—and some are not. I've come to realize that this is the Lord's way of arranging my life, and that the greatest delusion is to think that the two must be wholly congruent. This attractive delusion was the triple temptation Jesus rejected at the beginning of his ministry. And with his help, it is the temptation I hope to reject now in mine. The objects of my love need not be the sources of it, "for if you love those who love you, what reward will you have? Do not the Gentiles do as much?" (Matt. 5:46-47). But I have also found that those whom I once thought could only be objects can become sources if I can learn to take the risk of loving them. I have found, with John of the Cross, that "where there is no love, put love and you will find love."

So I thank God for the real body he has given me—

for its comely parts and its uncomely, for its lights and its shadows. It is the community that reminds me that I have not been orphaned—either by having no one who cares for me or—what would be worse—by having no one to care for. With its weight as well as with its weight-lifting power, the body of Jesus is a source of life for me. And I need to learn its body-languages.

SOUL LANGUAGE

The Lord Jesus has also left a most precious gift that speaks to my soul and mind. It is his Word. The word is intelligible speech—intelligible, at least, to those who have the mind of Christ (1 Cor. 2:16). The word gives shape and meaning to the bodily signs with which he comes to touch me. The word also gives shape to the powerful movement of the Holy Spirit within. It is indeed food. "Not by bread alone does man live but by every word that comes from the mouth of God" (Deut. 8:3).

The written word of ages past takes on a *now* meaning for me through the inspired preaching or teaching or prophecy in the Christian community. If the word is bread, it needs to be broken for me. And Jesus has provided his community with those especially anointed to break the loaves and distribute them. These may be the "shepherds and teachers" whom the Lord has anointed through the official ministry of the community (Eph. 4:11), or they may be those who in a habitual or even a passing way are moved by the Spirit to speak his word to the community and to me. In our day many media besides the spoken and the written word are available as channels of the ministry of the word, and none of them should be despised. The only real obstacle to my hearing the word through the many channels that are available to me is my lack of docility, my lack of listening, my lack of openness to hear. And that leads to the next gift that the Lord has given me, one of whose principal fruits is to open my ears to hear: the gift of the Holy Spirit.

SPIRIT LANGUAGE

What language does the Spirit speak? The word of the Scriptures? The word of the prophet? "Abba" and "Lord Jesus"? Yes, but—as will become clear in another chapter—that visible, intelligible, fully shaped human-divine word is only the terminus of a process. And even when that terminus does arrive, it is clear that the word does not circumscribe or exhaust the mystery it expresses. There is always more than the word can express, and the Spirit is the dynamic that guards and fosters the experience of the mystery (1 Cor. 2:7; 14:-2).

The mystery, of course, of God. The Spirit plumbs the depths of all things, even the depths of God (1 Cor. 2:10). But if, as the text says, there is a depth to *all* things, that surely includes my human self, of whose depths and mystery I become daily more and more aware. In modern terms, this would surely include the unconscious. For I am well aware that my deepest self goes beyond that of which I am consciously aware. My self is a totality, and part of the anguish of human existence is to find how limited are my channels of self-expression when I want to *totally* communicate, or when I want to express even partially some inward mystery of my self. I go to the funeral parlor to visit a close friend whose dearest one has died, and "words cannot express" what I want to say. At other times my joy is so great that I feel like only an explosion can release it. At other times I am troubled or depressed without knowing fully why—my "spirit" in all these cases looks for some way to process what it is experiencing, to "get it out." And rational speech just will not do. It is not the language of the Spirit.

Body language may help, for being symbolic as well as physically real, it lends itself to the expression of mystery; so I may dance or groan or do cartwheels or scream. A friend of mind finds that the routine of weaving is an outlet that even becomes a prayer and a healing experience.

But the New Testament, which teaches so emphatically that man is *spirit,* speaks also of a special gift of prayer by which man's spirit may be activated with a language of the spirit, enabling depth to speak unto depth (1 Cor. 14:2, 14). It is the gift of tongues (1 Cor. 12:10). It is not primarily a gift of communicating in a foreign language unknown to the speaker but known to the listener, though there have been reported instances of such effects, and the Pentecost account in Acts seems to be first of them (Acts 2:1-12). Rather, the gift is primarily non-rational prayer ("The one who speaks in a tongue speaks not to men but to God" 1 Cor. 14:2). Artless, it uses no phrenetic energy in formulation.

But *what* is it saying? The very question reveals perhaps the insatiable desire to comprehend and control the language, whereas Paul in Romans 8:26-27 sees the transcending of this control as the specific advantage of the language of the Spirit: "We do not know how to pray as we ought (i.e., what to say), but the Spirit himself intercedes for us with sighs too deep for words. And he who searches the hearts of men knows what the Spirit means, for the Spirit intercedes for the saints according to the will of God." Paul in this passage does give us this much of a clue, that the activity of the praying Spirit is, in part at least, intercession for one's own or others' needs. Elsewhere the activity is described as praising and thanking God (1 Cor. 14:16), the activity of the disciples on the first Pentecost when the Spirit descended upon them—they were telling of God's wonderful deeds in such an ecstatic way as to give scoffers occasion to accuse them of being drunk on new wine (Acts 2:11, 13).

But these aspects are only facets of the kind of mystery-language which tongues is: "He who speaks in tongues utters mysteries in the Spirit" (1 Cor. 14:2). The mystery of God, surely, but also the mystery of one's self—the unknown or half-known depths, which touched by the Spirit, begin to groan for the consummation of sonship. "The whole creation has been groaning in travail until now; and not only creation but we ourselves, who have the first fruits of the Spirit, groan inwardly as we await our full adoption as sons, the redemption of our bodies" (Rom. 8:22-23).

The processing of the chaotic depths is such an important activity of the prayer in the Spirit that it merits special treatment in a subsequent chapter. For the moment, suffice it to say that prayer in tongues is the Spirit's prelude to the Lord's Word. It enables me to discharge and process into praise the many forces in my depths that are hindering the Word from getting through. Once the Spirit has hovered over my chaos, and this I allow him to do when I pray in tongues, I am ready to hear the creative word—whether from the Bible as I open it to read, or from someone who speaks to me a "word of the Lord," or from some simple experience that tells me something of the Lord.

If it is the Bible I open, the word comes not like a quaint paragraph from an ancient book but like a personal letter received today from my best friend. This is what makes the scriptural word *prophecy*. It convicts me with a *now* meaning that changes my life. It is, like God's word to the prophet Jeremiah, a hammer shattering rock (Jer. 23:29). The rock it shatters is nothing other than my heart.

If it is a living human voice that ministers the word to me, this too is prophecy if it changes my life for the Lord. But this kind of prophecy can come to me also through an event, if through such an event I am converted and changed to know the Lord better and live his ways more honestly and joyfully.

I am, in fact, being daily bombarded by this word. The only reason I don't hear it is that I have not yielded sufficiently to the disposing Spirit.

That is one of the reasons why the Spirit-language of tongues is called a gift. Not that I am suddenly given a miraculous lingual mechanism—the mechanism is as simple as singing in the shower or humming a line of nonsense. But the gift is to let go inwardly and outwardly sufficiently to allow this foolishness of babbling praise to well forth. And this becomes the gift of one's personal prayer-language before God. The stumbling block to tongues for most is not its difficulty but its frightening simplicity. In the presence of the Father I must shed my adulthood and speak as freely as a babbling child.

"Why does the hummingbird hum?" begins an old joke. "Because he doesn't know the words." With childlike seriousness we might ask, why does the Spirit-filled Christian pray in tongues? Because he doesn't know the words—and because, furthermore, he knows the Father doesn't care, for the Father is not impressed with rhetoric but only with the language of the heart. And if the heart is speaking by the power of the Holy Spirit, then the one praying is sharing in the eternal mutual utterance of the Father and Son.

This suggests a second reason why tongue-prayer is a gift. As I yield to it, I become ever more conscious that I have stepped into a stream that was flowing long before I even approached the bank, and that as I enter the water, I am carried by a power other than my own. This may be obvious only to the one who has experienced it, but such is the awareness.

Then what does it take to receive the gift and to begin speaking the Spirit language of tongues? It takes the kind of letting go that a novice swimmer must do if he would learn to swim. He cannot continue to thrash the water. He has to learn to risk if he would discover how the water will support and carry him. So, too, I must turn to the Lord in a new way. I must begin walking toward him on the waters of faith, as Peter did (Matt. 14:22-23), and that means to let go of cherished securities—of heart-fists clenched in anger or possessiveness, or whatever else I am consciously clinging to that makes something other than the Lord my number one desire.

To be an authentic experience of the Spirit, yielding to tongues must be a new and radical way of proclaiming that Jesus is the Lord of my life. (For the Spirit leads us to confess and experience that Jesus is Lord, 1 Cor. 12:3). It demands conversion of life and a turning to the Lord. And yet, it is not a work, it is a gift. The asceticism it takes is not one of long and painful work, but simply the death to self it takes to truly receive the

49

Lord's gift, to believe in his love and his touch and his power enough to put out my hand and claim it. The difficulty is only in the utter simplicity of the act: to babble like a child.

To learn to speak the language of the Spirit is not to despise the languages of the mind or of the body but to make them most meaningful. The word, through the Spirit, becomes prophecy. And the body, through the Spirit, becomes the bridge of encounter that is completely human and completely Christian.

CHAPTER FOUR

The Spirit and the Word

One of the ways in which the gift of the Spirit can be recognized is through the insatiable hunger he gives us for the Word of God. Within three weeks after my secretary received the baptism in the Holy Spirit, her little copy of the New Testament was dog-eared and worn as if it were ten years old. Although by profession a scripture scholar, I must confess that the experience of the Holy Spirit has led me to listen to the word with an unprecedented attentiveness. The Word began to speak, in a way it never had before, to my daily experience.

This precious and mysterious relationship between the Spirit and the word deserves exploring. I invite you to travel with me back into the Old Testament for a meditative journey into the New, and to explore the phenomenon of prophecy, for it is there above all that the relationship of the Spirit and Word appears most clearly.

THE SPIRIT IN EARLY PROPHECY

The focus of the earliest Israelite prophecy was upon the spirit rather than the word—that is, what characterized early prophecy was less the intelligible message conveyed than the ecstatic seizure of the prophet and the wonders worked through him. In Numbers 11:- 10-30, a text of what the scholars call the Elohist tradition, we find a description of the prophetic phenomenon which anticipates Pentecost in a striking way. The people in the desert complain to Moses and cry out for food. Moses in turn complains to the Lord and says that the people are too heavy a burden for him to carry. The

Lord responds by telling Moses to assemble seventy of the elders of Israel and to bring them to the meeting tent:

> When they are in place beside you, I will come down and speak to you there, I will also take some of the Spirit that is on you and will bestow it on them, that they may share the burden of the people with you. You will then not have to bear it by yourself.

The Lord then rebukes the people for their lack of trust but also promises them an abundance of food. Moses wonders how enough meat could be found to feed such a multitude. To this the Lord answers, "Is this beyond the Lord's reach? You shall see now whether or not what I have promised you takes place." The text continues:

> So Moses went out and told the people what the Lord had said. Gathering seventy elders of the people, he had them stand around the tent. The Lord then came down in the cloud and spoke to him. Taking some of the Spirit that was on Moses, he bestowed it on the seventy elders, and as the spirit came to rest on them, they prophesied.
>
> Now two men, one named Eldad and the other Medad, were not in the gathering but had been left in the camp. They too had been on the list, but had not gone out to the tent; yet the spirit came to rest on them also, and they prophesied in the camp. So, when a young man quickly told Moses, "Eldad and Medad are prophesying in the camp," Joshua, son of Nun, who from his youth had been Moses' aide, said, "Moses, my lord, stop them!" But Moses answered him, "Are you jealous for my sake? Would that the Lord might bestow his spirit on them all!"

Four points are worth noting about this text: (1) Prophecy is attributed to the coming of the spirit upon the elders, and the Spirit is graphically described as being shared out from Moses upon the community of elders—in a way that will, of course, be fulfilled and transcended when the risen Lord, possessor of the Spirit from the Father, shares it with the early community of Jerusalem. (2) There is no indication of any intelligible word or message which the prophets utter. The experience seems to be rather one of raptured enthusiasm or mystic exaltation. (3) The spirit tends to overflow the structural program which the Lord himself has prescribed. Thus, in spite of the fact that Eldad and Medad do not come to the meeting (we don't know whether they were sick or whether they overslept or perhaps couldn't get a ride to the prayer meeting!), they too received the spirit—a reminder to Joshua and all other narrow-minded structuralists that while the Lord himself may institute a structure through which his spirit is to be bestowed, like the Church in later times, he does not thereby limit himself nor his spirit to that channel. (4) Moses expresses a desire, almost unthinkable by Old Testament standards, that all the people of the Lord might be prophets. There will be a great span of time between this statement in Numbers and the prophecy in Joel 3:1-5, and an even longer span to Acts 2, where Peter points to Pentecost as the fulfillment of the promise to pour out the Spirit upon the entire community. For the time being, let us simply note that in this very early text describing prophetic activity long before such writing prophets as Amos or Hosea or Isaiah, the focus is upon the spirit more than upon the word in moving the prophet.

It is the same with Samuel and his school of ecstatic prophets described in 1 Samuel 19:18-24. Pursued by Saul, David escapes to Samuel in the sheds near Ramah.

> When Saul was told that David was in the sheds near Ramah, he sent messengers to arrest David. But when they saw the band of prophets presided over by Samuel, in a prophetic frenzy, they too fell into the prophetic state. Informed of this, Saul sent

other messengers, who also fell into the prophetic state. For the third time Saul sent messengers, but they too fell into the prophetic state.

Saul then went to Ramah himself. Arriving at the cistern of the threshing floor on the bare hilltop, he inquired, "Where are Samuel and David?" and was told, "At the sheds near Ramah." As he set out from the hilltop toward the sheds, the spirit of God came upon him also, and he continued on in a prophetic condition until he reached the spot. At the sheds near Ramah he too stripped himself of his garments and he too remained in the prophetic state in the presence of Samuel; all that day and night he lay naked.

The last detail about Saul's being stripped simply means that he threw aside his regalia and lay before the Lord dressed as a prisoner or a slave. Throughout the whole passage you will note there is no indication of any intelligible word which the prophets utter. They are simply experiencing the spirit of the Lord in a highly non-verbal, non-rational manner.

Even when we come to the great prophets Elijah and Elisha, we find them more charismatic wonder workers and witnesses of the presence of the living God than preachers. That is why when Elisha is about to succeed Elijah, he asks *not* to be a faithful carrier of the *word* of Elijah but rather to be given "a double portion of your *spirit*" (2 Kings 2:9).

NEED FOR DISCERNMENT

From these texts we can conclude that in the tenth and the ninth centuries B.C. the Spirit of Yahweh was indeed the sign of the prophet and manifested itself ecstatically and in wonders. The prophets did, of course, occasionally speak out with directive prophecy, telling king or people what they should or should not do. It was not long, as we might guess, before prophets claiming to possess the spirit of Yahweh gave opposing directions. And thus when prophecy entered the arena of verbal messages, the problem immediately arose of discerning which prophet really was speaking in the name of the Lord. The crisis is dramatized in the clash between Ahab, the king of Israel, and the prophet Micaiah ben Imlah (1 Kings 22:1-40). Ahab sees an opportunity to seize Ramoth-gilead from the king of Aram and asks the help of Jehoshaphat, king of Judah, for the military undertaking. Jehoshaphat agrees but adds, "Seek the word of the Lord at once"—by which he simply means that the prophets should be consulted.

In those days there were bands or communities of prophets in Israel. The king gathers all of them together, in number about four hundred, and asks them, "Shall I go to attack Ramoth-gilead or shall I refrain?" The prophets unanimously urge the king to attack, promising victory. Jehoshaphat, however, wonders whether all available prophets have been consulted. He discovers that Ahab had brushed aside Micaiah ben Imlah precisely because Micaiah never prophesied to Ahab's liking. In a public showdown, the school of prophets led by Zedekiah repeat their urging to attack. Micaiah, however, replies that these prophets speak under the influence of a lying spirit; he prophesies disaster if the king carries out his plan of aggression. King Ahab summarily then throws Micaiah into prison and gallantly marches off to war—only to be slain on the battlefield.

Occurrences such as these gradually led the more enlightened of the nation to look for some norm by which to discern true prophecy other than the general claim to be moved by the Spirit of God. Thus arose a greater interest in the prophetic message—the *content* of which could be checked against the doctrinal traditions of Israel on the one hand and against the events of Israel's ongoing history on the other (Deut. 18:9-22). It began to be seen that the movement of the Spirit, if authentic, should normally lead to some clarity of vision, some message addressed to man's mind as well as to his heart and spirit.

THE WORD IN CLASSICAL PROPHECY

Thus when we come into the age of classical prophecy, beginning with Amos, we find almost a total disappearance of the expression, "the Spirit of the Lord came to so-and-so . . ." It is replaced by the expression, "the word of the Lord came to so-and-so . . ." The expression *the word of the Lord* occurs 241 times in the Old Testament, of which 221 or 93% occur in the prophetic writings. The more explicit expression is "The word of the Lord came to so-and-so," appearing 123 times. Note that the expression is not *"a* word came" but *"the* word came"—just as the previous tradition had spoken of *the* spirit and not *a* spirit coming upon the authentic prophet.

What then has begun to happen in the evolution of the prophetic experience? The word spirit, we know, comes from the Hebrew *ruah* and the Greek *pneuma.* It means basically breath or wind. The emphasis is upon movement, pregnant promise or sign of power, without much consideration of the direction that this movement or power will take. *Word,* on the other hand, suggests a more formulated shape to the movement of the spirit, a message or a directive. It is really the difference between man's breath thrust outward from his lungs and the shape given that breath when the tongue and lips form a word.

This is not to say that the Hebrew notion of *word* is static. For the Greek, *logos* is a descriptive word, a noetic word. When man forms a word in his mind or on his lips, he is taking the multiplicity of his experiences and putting them in order. Concepts do for man what pigeonholes do for a postal clerk—they give him slots to sort whatever comes within the range of his experience. Thus in his mind man can create an inner cosmos which, hopefully, will be a true picture of the outer world. The Hebrew *dabar* means word too, but in a much more dynamic sense. It comes from a root verb meaning *to drive, to get behind and push.* When the Hebrew speaks a word, he is not taking in the outside world and shaping it within himself. Rather he is thrusting something creative and powerful outward from himself into the external world and actually changing that world. The word assumes an almost independent existence. When Isaac mistakenly blessed Jacob instead of Esau, the word of blessing had gone forth from Isaac and he could not recall it. All he could do was to send out another blessing upon Esau, to neutralize or balance the effects of the first blessing.

GOD'S CREATIVE WORD

This view of reality may seem to us very simplistic, but it helps to prepare us to understand how God could actually *send* his word (Isa. 55:10-11) and how the word of the Lord spoken through the prophets was understood not only to describe the future event but to actually create it. God's word creates the future of his people. Such was the starting point of Israel's theology of creation. It began with the historical creation of a people and ended with cosmic creation, not the other way around. When the prophetic promise that Israel would return after exile was fulfilled, it involved the historical defeat of the vaunted creator-gods of Babylon, whose role in the cosmogenesis the Israelites had heard recited year after year at the Babylonian new year festival. But now the word of Yahweh had proved these gods to be wind and waste (Isa. 41:29). Clearly the word of the Lord had no limits to its power. It extended to the very creation of the cosmos.

It is upon this tradition that the priestly author in Genesis 1 shapes his fantastic description of the creation of the world by the word of God: "And God said, 'Let there be light. . . .' And God said. . . . And God said. . . .''

GOD'S CREATIVE SPIRIT

By this time, though, a new respect had been born for the notion of the *spirit*. Left aside for a while because it lacked the specific direction and controllability of a concrete message, the theology of the spirit begins to reappear as a vital thing with Ezekiel. Witness of the death of the nation in the Babylonian captivity, he was called to sound the promise of new life. For this purpose, the theology of the Spirit needed to be emphasized once again. The Spirit enters into Ezekiel and brings him to life as God's messenger (Ezek. 2:2). The Spirit is not tied to the temple in Jerusalem but is as mobile as wings and wheels (Ezek. 1:20); it follows the people into exile. The Spirit enters into the dry bones and brings them to life again—an obvious image of the people regenerated by the Spirit of the Lord (Ezek. 37:1-14; 36:25-26; see also Is. 44:3-4).

SPIRIT AND WORD

So if the pendulum has swung from spirit to word, it is now swinging back to center where spirit and word are seen to be inseparable elements in the renewal and regeneration of the people. We find the two concepts combined in Second Isaiah. How will he describe the magnificent historical event by which the Lord shatters the pride of Babylon and restores his people? He attributes the work both to the Spirit (breath) of the Lord and to his Word: "The grass withers, the flower wilts, when the *breath* (spirit) of the Lord blows upon it . . . The *word* of our God stands forever" (Is. 40:7-8).

All the preceding development has been building to the peak of the pyramid which appears now in the theology of the cosmic creation, attributed both to the *word* of God and to his *spirit* (Ps. 33:6). The relation of these two reaches its highest expression in Genesis 1: "In the beginning God created the heavens and the earth. The earth was waste and void, darkness covered the abyss, and the spirit of God hovered over the waters. Then God said, 'Let there be light . . .'" We have been so accustomed to reading this opening page of the Bible in terms of God's effortless creation of the universe from nothing, that we are likely to neglect the crucial importance of verse 2, which describes the spirit hovering over the chaos. The creative word which is first heard in verse 3 is prepared for by a description of the primeval chaos. It is darkness and watery formlessness. Over it God's spirit hovers. The Hebrew word for "hovers" suggests the action of a bird inclining over its nest and beating its wings in an effort to get its nestlings to fly. To what is formless, weak, and helpless it is addressed as an image of hope and promise. After the spirit has done its work of preparing and disposing, the creative word can enter the chaos and bring shape, order and beauty to it. The chaos can then hear obediently the word, "Let there be light." And there is light.

IN THE CHARISMATIC COMMUNITY

The relation of Spirit and Word in the Bible suggests a model for the rhythm of prayer and manifestations of the Spirit in the charismatic community. The first movement of prayer is surrender to the hovering Spirit. There need be no rush to put shape or form to prayer; it is better to let depth commune with depth. Thus, tongues ordinarily precedes prophecy or the word. After this preparatory work of the Spirit, the Word can enter with creative power to shape the community's life, to interpret what the Spirit has been doing in our spirit (Rom. 8:15), to make a beautiful universe from elements as yet unformed and unshaped. So, too, in the Pentecost experience, Peter's interpretive sermon (Acts 2:14-39) gives the word meaning of the tongues phenomenon which preceded it.

That is also why after praying in tongues, we should wait upon interpretation (1 Cor. 14:27-28). In private prayer, the word of the Lord is sometimes offered by a Scripture text to which one turns. In the praying community the word is furnished by interpretation or prophecy, or sometimes too by a Scripture text. The word therefore becomes most meaningful when it has been prepared by the work of the Spirit. The Spirit, on the other hand, looks to the word as the normal terminus of its work. Spirit then is related to word as pregnancy is to birth. In the concrete prayer experience, the work of the Spirit is frustrated if it does not end in the word. Or again, the work of the Spirit is like the inspiration of a melody; it does not reach its fullest meaning until words are put to it.

SPIRIT AND WORD IN THE NEW TESTAMENT

In what we have elaborated above, we have drawn primarily from the Old Testament. But the New Testament evidence confirms the same relationship between word and spirit. Matthew wrote his Gospel for a community that was divided in its charismatic leadership. That there were prophets in the Matthean community is obvious from the various references to them in his Gospel. But inasmuch as "false prophets" had already arisen, it was necessary to appeal to some other norm than the Spirit to discern the Spirit. Matthew's solution for discerning the Spirit in his community was to return to the *word* of Jesus. Therefore he wrote a Gospel that collected primarily the sayings of Jesus, which he compiled into five or six major discourses. In any dispute the word of Jesus is a command that is final (Matt. 28:20).

In consigning the word of Jesus to writing and to official publication Matthew did what Isaiah and Jeremiah did occasionally in Old Testament times (Is. 8:16-18; 30:8-15; Jer. 36). As long as their words were unwritten, Isaiah and Jeremiah felt they must continue repeating them orally. At length, when no one would listen to them, they consigned the message to writing as a perpetual memorial of what they had said. They then considered themselves discharged of their duty to preach that particular word. They could not have had this conviction unless they were persuaded that the word, though written, continued to be alive and pregnant with meaning even for the generations yet unborn.

But this raises a further problem; what assurance is there that the later generation will understand the word or allow it to touch them in a life-giving way? What assurance is there that for future generations the word once spoken or written will be anything more than a curious museum piece? The answer is that the Spirit must again be alive to give understanding to the word.

It is John's Gospel above all that develops this dimension of the Spirit-Word dynamic. After Jesus' long discourse on the Eucharist, in which he flatly declares that those who believe in him must eat his flesh and drink his blood, John records, "After hearing his words, many of his disciples remarked, 'This sort of talk is hard to endure. How can anyone take it seriously?' " In his answer Jesus replies, "It is the Spirit that gives life; the flesh is useless. The *words* that I spoke to you are *spirit* and life." Thus he emphasized that without a special gift of the Father, the words of Jesus are meaningless or absurd. Then he goes on to say, "This is why I have told you that no one can come to me unless it is granted him by my Father." At this point many of his disciples leave him. The Twelve, however, stay, and Peter explains, "Lord, to whom shall we go? You have the *words* of eternal life" (John 6:60-68).

This little incident is a dramatization of the principle laid down in the discourse at the Last Supper in which Jesus says that the role of the Spirit is to lead the believer into the full truth about Jesus, to make understandable his word (John 16:13).

Paul had already indicated this direction in 1 Corinthians 2:2-16. "We have received God's Spirit in order to be able to recognize the gifts he has given to us."

From this, we can conclude that if the Spirit precedes the word in its first coming to the prophet or the prophetic community, the Spirit also follows the word by giving understanding to the hearer. Perhaps it would be more precise to say the relationship in the listener is exactly what it is in the prophet, in which the Spirit always precedes the word. For the word which the listener hears prior to the activity of the Spirit is merely a human word like any other. Without the Spirit, the word, whether written in the Bible, read from the Bible, or preached from the pulpit, is no different from any other word in any other book or from any other mouth in the world. It is known simply noetically or at best esthetically. But it is not known as the word of God. It may entertain and enrich the listener but it does not convert and recreate him. It does not do what the word did for and through Jeremiah—tear down and build up, root up and plant (Jer. 2:10). Even for the Christian who theoretically accepts the Bible as the word of God, a given passage may at this particular moment be saying nothing to him if he has not opened himself first to the disposing work of the Spirit.

And so in some way it is always true that the work of the Spirit precedes that of the word. For even when my ears hear the sounds of the human word, the divine word is not born in my heart until the Lord's Spirit has hovered over me, as he hovered over Mary to bring about the enfleshment of the Word in person.

There is perhaps a further consequence that we can draw from this relationship. The Spirit is related to the word as heat is to light. Heat is felt; light is seen. In striving to bring God to others, it is more important to warm them by the love of God poured into our hearts (Rom. 5:5) than it is to blind them with more light than they can take at the moment. Thus real evangelization would be to offer to the spiritually sick a love that would hover over their chaos with enough listening and patience to prepare a receptive heart for the healing word.

Finally, the movements of the Spirit and the understanding and the sharing of the word are more than theological niceties. They are the very dynamic by which we come to experience the Spirit of God, who is a person; the Word of God, who is a person; and the Father to whom the Spirit and the Word lead. The Father offers us his word and gives us his Spirit that we might hear with our ears and understand with our heart (Is. 6:10). Moved by the Spirit, we know the Word for who he is, the Father's only-begotten. And that means to experience the Father as Jesus himself experiences him (John 14:9). Reading the Scripture in the Spirit, or praying and listening in the Spirit in the prayer meeting is an experience of the trinitarian life of God himself.

Can we say it more simply? Lovers have many ways

of expressing their love, but especially two. One is the word, "I love you." The other is the kiss. God's word to me, reduced to essence, is "I love you." His Spirit, as the mystics long ago observed, is his kiss. And the Baptism in the Holy Spirit? That's simply allowing myself to be kissed.

CHAPTER FIVE

The Spirit and the Creative Use of Chaos

Chaos or disorder is part of our daily experience, and we need to discover how to deal with it. We observe it in the world around us. The poverty of the world is nothing short of a nightmare. The civic peace of our neighborhoods is being invaded more and more by violence. Drug abuse is kidnaping our teenagers right out from under us. And in the church, the old structures that used to give us a sense of common identity and security have disappeared.

This external chaos is, however, not half so threatening as the internal chaos we experience—assuming that we allow ourselves to experience it. The chaos of the past, for example: in the last twenty-four hours there are some things I did but wish now I hadn't done; things I didn't do but now wish I had done. And anxieties and guilt feelings of this kind extend back through every twenty-four hours of my life. Life, I find, is not like a tape recording; I can't go back and try it over. I have to live with the mistakes. All I have now is my memory of the past, and that memory is a very present and active thing. I may experience much of it as pleasant, but there is also a lot of it that is chaotic.

The chaos of my present: when I admit it, I am really not in control of much of my life. I am a Charlie Brown who is not in control of the score, the batter, or even of his own team. And my kite is forever getting hung in a tree. The question here is not whether I should try to get control of the world around me; the question is what do I do with my own feelings of frustration at my lack of success in my attempts?

There there is the chaos about my future: how am I going to face that situation I've been trying to avoid for weeks? How am I going to get my work done in the little time I have? How will that other person respond to my attempts to straighten out a bad situation—will he accept my proposal or will he blast my head off?

If I reflect on this phenomenon of chaos long enough I realize that the chaotic elements in my life of which I become aware are only the surface of a sea whose depths I've never plumbed: my unconscious. God only knows what's down there. Once in a while my dreams give me an insight into the abyss, but I have the distasteful suspicion that what's down there infinitely surpasses what I've come to see on the surface. And that realization makes me feel even more that I'm on a roller coaster I can't guide, stop, or jump from.

RESPONSE TO CHAOS

To the experience of chaos there are many ways of reacting. One easy stratagem is to deny the chaos I'm in, to suppress, or to try to suppress, my awareness of it, to pretend to myself and to others that I'm the "cool cat" who really knows what's up, who's got a handle on everything, who is dismayed by nothing. The only problem with suppressing this kind of awareness is that, like any suppression, it ultimately takes its revenge. And I get the distinct feeling that the more I take this tack, the more I am really out of touch with what is going on; and others seem to sense it too. And so I end up in loneliness and frustration. In a community situation, I came across as one who has the answers ahead of time and really doesn't listen to the question.

Another tack is to react with power and control, that is, to yield to the compulsive drive to get this mess under control at any cost. This may manifest itself in a passion or a pretense to understand at once what's going on, or to control it with laws and enforcement mechanisms, to use the tantrum technique, to threaten to "walk out" of the situation, or to resort to threats and violence. This reaction is basically fear. I want to get control of or to eliminate what I do not comprehend. I don't want to be forced to ask myself any more questions. The problem with this approach is, of course, that I have defined my existence as a static one, and change is a threat. My ideals, even my religious ones, are defined more in terms of "plateau perseverance" than in terms of inward growth. And needless to say, in a "dialogue" situation this reaction only increases the chaos a community has to deal with.

Another option is to admit the mess but to project it away from myself where I can laugh at it at a safe distance. So I can entertain myself and others by pointing out and poking fun at the chaos in third parties. I enjoy Charlie Brown as long as I can call him by some other name than my own.

BIBLICAL RESPONSE

All of these options are attempts to escape from chaos rather than to look at it honestly and somehow to integrate it into my total experience. The Bible offers an option of dealing with chaos that is positive and healthy. Not only does it accept chaos as an inevitable prelude to new life, but it has a positive and practical theology for dealing with it in hope and love.

The primordial type of chaos appears, of course, in the second verse of the book of Genesis, the primeval chaos that preceded creation: "In the beginning God created the heavens and the earth. The earth was waste and void, darkness covered the abyss, and the spirit of God hovered over the waters." Prior to introducing the creative and shaping word ("And God said, 'Let there be light . . .'"), the author wishes to do justice to a process. Had he skipped the reference to chaos, the reader might think that the Lord's creative word had nothing to work on, but this is not so. We have perhaps been so indoctrinated to think of this passage as inculcating a creation *ex nihilo* that we overlook the fact that the first creative word *follows* the description of chaos and the hovering of the spirit of God. Theologically, the sequence is critical: the creative word comes as a resolution of the unresolved. Before it, the earth is *tohu wabohu*, two assonant words to suggest both emptiness and disorder; and the primeval watery abyss is covered with darkness. The combination of these images reveals the author's attempt to describe chaos in terms of a void, a disorder, formless water and darkness. Note that the chaos is not described as evil; it simply has not yet been shaped into the order that will bring the divine judgment that it is *good*. Quite simply, the chaos is possibility. But more than that, the Spirit of God is hovering over this chaos. And that means the chaos is more than possibility; it is *promise*.

For the exegetical readers who prefer the translation "mighty wind" instead of "spirit of God," I would like to point out that this masterpiece of priestly theology is built on the tradition of Ezekiel and probably also Second Isaiah, for whom the thought of the Spirit of God hovering over chaos was thoroughly congenial. Ezekiel sees God's spirit coming upon dry bones scattered on a desert plain and bringing them back to life (Ezek. 36-37). Second Isaiah sees both God's spirit and his word as agents of a new creation (Isa. 40:7-8; 42:1; 44:3-4). So too the priestly author is not interested in satisfying the scientists' curiosity about the sequence of events at the first creation. He is presenting his drama of creation from a theological viewpoint: it is the paradigm for all the creative and redeeming work of God throughout the whole of sacred history. Addressed to man, the Bible is interested in the cosmic creation only insofar as it reveals something about man and his relationship with God, his fellow man, and the world. So the element of chaos in Genesis is only as it were a primordial type for the other experiences of chaos common to man. Chaos of any type can be transformed into promise if the Spirit of God is allowed to hover over it; and when the Spirit has hovered sufficiently, the chaos can hear in obedience the word saying, "Let there be light."

PRAYER

Since the Spirit hovers over the primeval chaos and the word follows it, one of the principal contexts in which man's experience of chaos is worked out is, as we might have suspected, prayer. The Psalms frequently reveal man's "primal scream" in the face of his anxieties. The strong dosage of lament in the Psalms is a reminder to us that it is sometimes more important to get out the garbage within us than it is to mouth formulas. Psalm 22, beginning with the words, "My God, my God, why have you forsaken me?" is a good illustration of the chaos-to-cosmos process. It is a long "primal scream" that, when it is spent, becomes resolved into praise. Psalm 10 is another example. The Psalmist pours out his chaotic plight to the Lord, finally being comforted in his act of faith: "Thou dost see; yea, thou dost note trouble and vexation, that thou mayest take it into thy hands" (Ps. 10:14). If psalms such as these have something to say about the rhythm of prayer, perhaps they are telling us that our prayers are just too formal and nice if they prevent the primal volcano within us from spending itself first so that we may then be able to hear the other voice which is that of God.

Job follows the same pattern. His friends typify the school of "plateau perseverance." They try desperately to suppress Job's primal scream and even his theological question. Their static categories are adequate and sacred. The only problem is that they are not dealing with Job where he is. And hence the only "word" that resolves the chaos comes from him who, in the end, has been the one hovering over it all: the Lord who speaks from the chaotic whirlwind.

IN THE NEW TESTAMENT

How does the New Testament deal with chaos? If it is true that Matthew's version of the miracle stories tends to play down the "travailing prelude" to Jesus' mighty works in order to give place to his effortless *word,* there is plenty of other evidence that there was a manifestation of the chaotic before the release of power from him to heal.

Sometimes this was in Jesus himself. Before curing the deaf-mute with the word *ephphatha,* Jesus groans (Mark 7:34). In the Lazarus story, John mentions twice that Jesus "was troubled in spirit, moved by the deepest emotions," (John 11:33, 38), and in each case the movement prepares for a positive turn of events in a word from Jesus. Similarly, at the beginning of the passion, Jesus experiences great sorrow "even unto death" (Mark 14:34f.; Matt. 26:37f.). Although Luke does not report this detail, it is he alone who describes Jesus' prayer in the garden as an agony leading to sweat like blood (Luke 22:44). Once this is over, Jesus seems to experience an unearthly freedom and power as he is led through his torture. It is the fulfillment at the end of Jesus' ministry of the prophetic drama which inaugurated it; the temptation in which the spirit of Jesus is tested, being resolved in the three-fold word of the Scriptures.

If the "chaotic" in Jesus himself is not always reported, the unleashing of the chaotic in others is recorded often. And this leads us to some considerations on that special way in which the chaotic appears in the ministry of Jesus: the demonic. Quite frequently the approach of Jesus stirs up and brings out the chaotic. Mark's report of Jesus' first mighty work in Galilee is the cure of a demoniac in the synagogue. The first reaction to Jesus is shrieking and convulsions (Mark 1:23, 26). So too with the demoniac at Gerasa across the sea (Mark 5:7), where the chaotic extends even to the stampeding of the pigs over the cliff (Mark 5:13). The reaction is particularly strong in the case of the epileptic boy: at the sight of Jesus the spirit seizes the boy, convulsing him and making him roll around on the ground and foam at the mouth and shout (Mark 9:20, 26). Mark is especially interested in these details, because for him Jesus is the mightier one who challenges Satan in his stronghold, which is the dark, unknown side of man, source of so many of man's constrictions and fears. Satan may be the strong man who keeps his house well guarded, but Jesus is the stronger man announced by the Baptist (Mark 1:7) who by casting out the demonic in the power of the Holy Spirit has bound the strong man (Mark 3:22-30). In other words, Jesus is Lord not only of the areas of human life in which man knows some control (Mark 5:25-34) but also of those dark unknown areas that often paralyze him. The confession "Jesus is Lord" means that he is Lord of all that too (Phil. 2:10). That is, the ultimate in man's experience of the chaotic, the demonic, is no longer a completely uncharted abyss. The disciple may not know the measurements of that unknown, but he at least knows who is Lord of it, and the one in whose presence the chaotic can be tamed and cosmified: Jesus, the man of the Spirit. Mark sees even the debates of Jesus with his enemies and even his own disciples as an encounter with the demonic (the snares of his questioners are "temptations," and Peter even assumes the role of Satan, Mark 8:33). But to the extent that the disciple experiences the Spirit of Jesus, he can, like his Lord, actually challenge the demonic to come forth, whether this be in individuals or in society. The fears that keep others from stirring up the chaotic do not hold him back, for like Jesus, he sees in the chaotic not an enemy to be fled from but a land of promise to be claimed.

TONGUES AND CHAOS

Perhaps for this reason certain elements of the early Church's life and prayer reveal a quite positive use of the prelogical or, if you will, of the chaotic and the unformed. Carrying the lament-to-praise rhythm of the Psalms a step farther, the early Church would experience a kind of nonrational prayer which Paul describes as praying in tongues. If the Pentecost experience as described by Luke indicates that the exuberance of tongues was the result of ecstatic joy (Acts 2), there is also evidence that this form of nonrational prayer could voice the more chaotic, dark and anxious side of the Christian experience. In Romans 8:22-27, Paul describes the Christian life and prayer as a *groaning*. He says first that all creation groans and is in agony even until now. Then he adds, "We too who have the first-fruits of the Spirit, groan inwardly while we await the redemption of our bodies." And then he proceeds to explain the relation of the Spirit to the Christians' yet unfulfilled expectations: "The Spirit too helps us in our weakness, for we don't know how to pray as we ought; but the Spirit himself makes intercession for us with groanings that cannot be expressed in speech. He who searches the hearts knows what the Spirit means, for the Spirit intercedes for the saints as God himself wills."

So groaning is attributed to creation, to the Christian, and to the Spirit. The Greek word for groaning here is exactly what it was in Mark 7:34, Jesus' groaning prior to his curing the deaf-mute. It is obvious that Paul is accepting as normal in prayer at least this much of the chaotic, that we do not know how to pray as we ought. We can conclude from this that an anxiety to be in rational control of our experience of God or of our conversation with him is not even a Christian ambition. It is not necessary nor even desirable. It would seem to me that Paul is here implicitly inviting the Christian in prayer to go deeper than the rational on the one hand, and higher than it on the other. *Deeper:* groaning suggests the expression of deep desire to release the power of the unconscious, which is, precisely, not fully conscious nor understandable. In some way this may correspond to what he says in 1 Corinthians 14:2, that he who prays in tongues "utters mysteries in the Spirit," the mystery of God, surely, but also the mystery of the self. *Higher*: such an activity might be dangerous and simply destructive were it not directed toward a resolution somehow in something or someone higher than self. The biblical paradigm of the Spirit hovering over the chaos seems to correspond to this polarity quite well. Christian prayer as groaning is a bringing of the chaotic to the over-hovering of the Holy Spirit.

When the Lord led me to a new life in the Spirit, I began to realize he had also given me a power to deal with chaos which I had not experienced before. For years my prayer life lacked vitality and real conversion power. Very little seemed to be happening in my life. And it was not for lack of effort. I came to prayer very much as I came to any other human activity. The first thing to do, I thought, was to establish order, to put distractions aside, to suppress the garbage floating around inside me so that I could "get on with the agenda." Then I tried to think about God and turned to the Scripture for help. But it did not speak to me at any converting heart-depth. At most I was impressed with the esthetics of the word, not with its power to divide bone from marrow and soul from spirit (Heb. 4:12). I see now that I was trying to cap the pressures of my unconscious under the lid of a manhole on which I then tried to stand and pray. But my balance was constantly being upset because those powers would simply not stay down there. They insisted on pushing the manhole cover off and crawling out, much to my distress, and much, I thought, to the detriment of my prayer life. I did not know or even suspect that they could, by the power of God's spirit, become the raw material for a kind of prayer that would heal me in those very depths.

But that is, precisely, I have found, what praying in the Spirit makes possible to happen. I let myself go in praise of the Lord. As I pour forth his praise in tongues, not knowing what I am saying but only knowing that I am praising him, I am aware that my own depths are being opened and I begin to see passing by the screen of my consciousness the images of fears, anxieties, remorse, as well as joys—which I hardly suspected were down there. I am not frightened by them, and I do not try to stop them at the threshold of consciousness to analyze or suppress them. For they are part of the very chaos which the Holy Spirit is converting into praise. I release them and let them go up, however chaotically, however volcanically, in praise of the Lord. My focus is not these chaotic forms and pressures themselves, but the Lord whose Spirit of love is taking them and recycling them into praise. One day the mystery of what was happening in this new form of prayer came to me in these words:

My son, my praise is the only mirror in which you can see rightly yourself and all that is in you, and all that is. For years you have stood like a sentry at the gate of your dark depths, checking, analyzing, and sometimes repressing these things within you. I have been leading you to see that in my presence you must let go of that pretended control and simply pour out my praise. If anxieties, problems, or even questionable thoughts or desires surface as you pray, turn them all over to me in praise. For as you let them go toward me, you will for the first time see their back side, you will begin to see their root. Till now you have been cutting off only the surface growth—and they have grown back as quickly as you cut. But when you turn totally to me, you can begin to see them totally, and this seeing is the beginning of your healing.

Once I allow the Spirit sufficient time to hover over this chaos, I find myself in a state of awareness and listening so calm and intense that when I open the Scripture, the Word seems to literally boom out at me with the awesome tenderness and power that only the Lord's word could have. Or it may just be his presence that is the word to me. Or it may come in a more specific way, like the "prophecy" I shared above. However the word may come, I feel its healing and cosmifying power. What has made the difference? The preceding work of the Spirit preparing my chaos for the Word of the new creation.

A further fruit of this gift has been a greater confidence in facing and healing the chaotic in others. Less fearful of it in myself, I am less fearful of it in others. To help the other lovingly to surface the chaotic is the first step in the ministry of deliverance, a casting out of the forces that hold him bound. In some cases, where the other is so bound that he seems to have no more rational or Christian self-possession at all, direct confrontation and exorcism may be called for. But in most cases, it is simply to try to minister to the other the same kind of hovering-over which the Lord ministers to me: the love that is all warmth, tenderness, and liberating listening. That is why the ministry of deliverance is not one of human might or power but the work of the Lord's Spirit (Zech. 4:6). Above all there is no place in it for spiteful anger, for "the anger of man does not achieve the righteousness of God" (James 1:20).

And I have felt called to this ministry not only with individuals but also with groups, especially with my own community. Less anxious to have an immediate solution and control the behavior of others through externally imposed expectations, I find myself much more willing to let the chaotic depths surface so that they can be dealt with lovingly. I find myself less fearful that someone will say the wrong thing, for I feel myself overshadowed by that loving Spirit whose creative power no chaos escapes and who knows how to make all things work together unto the good of those who love him (Rom. 8:28). I am beginning to understand how to allow the cosmifying power of the light to await, as Mary did, the womb-dark work of the Spirit. The good news is even better than I thought: no chaos is too much for the Holy Spirit. For him, it is the very stuff of the new creation!

CHAPTER SIX

Body Ministry

We now return to body language. In a previous chapter we saw how it is the Father's plan that we discover the Spirit in the body which is the community and enter into the kind of body language which it speaks, primarily the sacraments. There the emphasis was on the acceptance in faith of our own bodiliness and the bodiliness of the Lord's way of coming to us. As the Spirit moves more and more powerfully in our lives we discover that there is much more to this body language than simple receptivity. As the Lord Jesus touches us through the power of his Spirit, he anoints us for action, for a bodily ministry to others within the community and without. As we yield more and more to this ministry, the life of the Spirit grows in us. The body languages which we need to learn, and which are given us by the Spirit to be developed in and for the body are four: witness, service, healing, and fasting.

WITNESS

"You shall receive power when the Holy Spirit shall come upon you, and you shall be my witnesses . . . to the end of the earth" (Acts 1:8). I know that this word is addressed to me as really as it was addressed to the first community of disciples. I know too that it is to me as much as to the first disciples that Jesus says: "You are the light of the world. A city set upon a hill cannot be hid, nor do men light a lamp and put it under a bushel but on a stand so that it gives light to all in the house. Let your light so shine before men that they may see your

75

good works and give glory to your Father who is in heaven" (Matt. 5:14-16).

It has been said that the saints are the footnotes of the Gospel. The saints that I have read about, and more particularly the saints that I have known, were more than that. They were the Good News made visible: the Word made flesh in a human life that spoke to me like thunder. All the books that I have read and all the sermons that I have heard have never moved me so powerfully nor made me feel the touch of the Lord so closely as the encounter with a brother or a sister whom the Lord has touched. This tells me that authentic Christian experience is somehow God's word itself. Perhaps this is what the Scripture means when it says, "All that is illumined by light becomes light" (Eph. 5:13). If others' Christian experience has been so powerful in moving me, then I wonder if part of the very healing of the Lord that has worked in my life is not to "go home to your friends and tell them how much the Lord has done for you and how he has had mercy on you" (Mark 5:-19). That was the word of Jesus to him from whom he had driven the legion of demons, and his word to me could hardly be different.

It would seem only normal to want to share with others what the Lord has done in our lives. Oddly, though, I find in many of my fellow Christians, and often in myself, a reluctance to do this. Somehow I still find myself tempted to believe that Jesus is only for my private and personal life, that he is not something to be shared. Sometimes the thought comes more subtly, suggesting that the deepest secrets of my heart are to be shared only with God and perhaps with one or the other understanding friend. And is there not danger that this sacred experience might be scoffed at and rejected—and even Jesus himself said not to scatter my pearls before swine. But I know that is only a half-truth, for every time that I have risked laying before others what Jesus has done in my life, it has moved them powerfully. I feel then the joy of having yielded to the Spirit, but my joy is tinged with a bit of regret for the times I listened to excuses and withheld my witness. The truth of Jesus' word comes home to me: "So everyone who acknowledges me before men, I also will acknowledge before my Father who is in heaven; but whoever denies me before men I also will deny before my Father who is in heaven" (Matt. 10:32-33).

Real witnessing, I find, is both harder and easier than preaching. There are those well-intentioned Bible enthusiasts who go about pointing to the Bible and telling others what they should do, but that is not witnessing. Witnessing is doing just what Jesus told the healed man to do: "Go and tell what the Lord has done for *you.*" Witnessing does not mean, then, telling others what they should do for the Lord, but simply sharing what the Lord has done for me. And that takes a lot more willingness to put myself on the line than it takes just to speak words. On the other hand, witnessing is easier than preaching, for while men can argue about ideas, they cannot argue with my experience. They may not care to identify with it, but they cannot deny that it is mine, and that something has happened to me. If the Lord has really changed my life physically or mentally or emotionally or spiritually, then I have a miracle to talk about, a sign of the Lord's living power today. That sign may not of itself produce faith in him who witnesses it, any more than it did in the ministry of Jesus, but it is the best sign the Lord has to give—and the best sign I can give. It is truly amazing that when Jesus was asked for a sign from heaven, he said that the only sign to be given was the sign of Jonah, for as the pagan Ninevites converted and found new life at the preaching of Jonah, so would it be with those who would convert and believe at the preaching of Jesus (Luke 11:29-32). From then on, the greatest sign that Jesus offers the world is what happens in the lives of those who come to believe in him.

But it is obvious from this also that my attitudes and actions will give credibility to what I say in witness. If the Spirit has truly touched me, then the fruits of the Spirit will be obvious in my life, and it will not take many words to explain where they come from: love, joy, peace, patience, kindness, goodness, fidelity, gentleness, and self-control (Gal. 5:22).

SERVICE

One of the greatest signs that Jesus has touched and healed me is that I am now capable in a new way of serving others. This is the second kind of body language. The effect of Jesus' healing touch on Peter's mother-in-law was her rising to serve them (Mark 1:31). It is in this way that I show myself to be a true disciple of Jesus: "Whoever would be great among you must be your servant, and whoever would be first among you must be slave of all. For the Son of Man also came not to be served but to serve, and to give his life as a ransom for many" (Mark 10:45).

Intellectual that I am, I have always tended to think my most important contribution to be in the area of ideas. Is it not true service to enlighten my fellow men? And I have even felt this tendency in evaluating my contribution to my own community: is not my greatest contribution to do those things which other people cannot do? But the wisdom of Jesus at length has overtaken me. On the night before he died, when he had so little time to share his final teachings with his disciples, he said not a word at all. He simply rose from the table, laid aside his outer garments, girded himself with a towel, and began washing the feet of his disciples. It was a job that anyone could have done, and ordinarily it was done by a slave. Little wonder that Peter should react. Jesus was Lord and Master, but he was doing something that just anyone can do. That was precisely the point: in the company of Jesus' disciples, the truly great service is to do for one another those things, which, because they are earthly and monotonous, because just anybody can do them, often don't get done.

It is on these works of love, done without "checking out" those for whom we do them, that we will be judged to be the chosen sheep, that is, disciples worthy of hearing the Lord's word, "Come, you blessed of my Father, possess the kingdom prepared for you from the foundation of the world" (Matt. 25:31-46).

And yet in the Christian experience we are called to serve not for the sake of service, but because our eyes are focused upon the person of the Lord and the person of the brother or sister we are serving. I have at times fallen victim of the heresy—rather the idolatry—that work is God. The Lord may call us to serve and to work, but he remains our Lord and he forbids us to put service or work upon his throne in his stead. But I have known communities where this has happened—such a high priority was put on work that celebration and prayer became marginal concerns. Because the members of the community measured their expectations of one another in terms of service, community living became not a sharing of Jesus and his love but an alienating burden of demands. Such service bore little witness to the Lordship of Jesus. I must never allow myself to forget that the Lord who called himself servant, who invites me to become servant with him, is the only one who can teach me how to serve and be refreshed in service.

One retreat day I was quite depressed with what I considered the pedestrian pace of my community in the life in the Spirit. There was perhaps a lot of self-righteousness in my feelings about my brothers, but I felt that they were simply not yielding to the Spirit. That evening I was moved to visit one of them who was ill in bed. As I simply let myself *be* there for him, listening to him and striving to bring him courage and joy, I felt a tremendous peace settle over me, a peace I knew came only from the Lord. I had learned that it was this gesture of love and simple service that the Lord wanted of me rather than the not-quite-Christian impatience by which I expected everyone (else!) to be perfect. Truly, the supreme body language is to serve.

HEALING

Impressed as we have been from our earliest childhood with the miracle of medicine and wonder drugs, it is quite possible that the only context in which we can imagine healing, of the body at least, is the doctor's office, the hospital bed, or the medicine cabinet. And indeed we can only thank God for the ministry of medicine. Even in New Testament times the early Church counted among its ministers a doctor (Col. 4:14), though it was also aware of the limitations of the science and the art (Mark 5:25-26). Yet it is remarkable that the most skillful of physicians will tell us that the mental and spiritual attitude of the patient is as important an ingredient in his recovery as the medicine he may take. This general observation is further buttressed by the fact that well over half of the hospital beds in this country are occupied by persons suffering from illnesses that are mental, emotional, or psychosomatic.

Now if man is an interacting organism of body, soul, and spirit, then surely authentic Christian ministry is a vocation to healing, and the resources of the Spirit are there to be tapped for their usefulness in healing the whole person. This insight is very biblical, for the Old Testament notion of holiness is basically wholeness, and if the Christian life here in this world is an anticipation of the Resurrection, then there is nothing magical or weird or esoteric about feeling the effects of the risen life of Christ even physically. Many passages of the Gospel reflect this view; the most striking is perhaps that of the cure of the paralytic (Mark 2:1-12; Matt. 9:2-8; Luke 5:18-26). Confronted by a paralytic let down through the roof, Jesus first ministers to the man's spirit, with the words, "My son, your sins are forgiven." When Jesus' ability to forgive sins is challenged, he proceeds to heal the man physically: "Stand up! Pick up your mat and go home." One of the most precious body ministries with which the community of Jesus has been endowed is the healing brought to the body through the ministration of the Spirit.

The difference between this kind of healing and autosuggestive healing or magic should be obvious. The latter represents an attempt to get control of the powers of the supernatural, often through esoteric means—an attitude for which the Bible has utter disdain and revulsion.

God is not someone available through manipulation: "I will be who I will be," he says to Moses when Moses asks his name (Exod. 3:14). The Lord is a person with sovereign and infinite freedom. To know him is to feel the effect of his power and his healing, but one does not extort healing from God as one operates a slot machine. Healing can come when we focus not upon the healing of God but upon the God of healing. This basically means that we surrender to God's plan of salvation, the supreme expression of which is given in the Lord's Prayer: "Hallowed be thy name, thy kingdom come, thy will be done on earth as it is in heaven." It is to open ourselves first of all to responding to the person of God and his goodness, to praise him for the glory of his grace shown to us, and to commit ourselves totally to his loving plan of salvation, the accomplishment of his will. Far from being resignation to the status quo ("Thy will be done" never means that!), it is a total surrender to the invading warmth of his recreative love. "Thy will be done" is not a shamefaced retreat before the inevitable, it is an aggressive claim of God's salvation for our unredeemed human experience. It means exactly the same thing as "Thy kingdom come."

Human suffering and illness is an excellent context in which to pray, "Thy kingdom come." It means we take the whole person, body, soul, and spirit, and consciously surrender him to the saving will of God. We need to do this with all our human experience, but illness and physical need provide a most common and obvious occasion. It may be a stumbling block for us, for it takes more faith to believe that the Lord can touch us physically than to believe that he can cure us in spirit. But where in Scripture do we find any basis for limiting God's power and for presuming on our own that a physical cure is *not* his will? Why should we limit God's power by thinking he cannot or will not cure in this specific instance? If he decides not to, that is his business; but not to ask is a lack of faith. If we do not witness any immediate physical effect, we know that, at least if we have prayed in faith, we have put the person and his need into a completely new frame of reference, into the coming of God's kingdom, so that it becomes consciously one of those things which we now let the Lord turn to good (Rom. 8:28). It is true that those who never ask for healing will never be disappointed. But neither will they ever experience how really good the Good News can be.

So too, Jesus himself did not hesitate to petition that the cup of the passion be taken from him, even saying to the Father, "All things are possible to thee" (Mark 14:36). When it became evident that the Father willed that his Son drink that cup, and Jesus said, "Thy will be done" (Matt. 22:42), the event took on a totally different significance; Jesus' surrender was not mere passive resignation and acceptance. This was the positive, saving event that would bring about the coming of the kingdom. Jesus' prayer had not been futile; his prayer *was heard* (Heb. 5:7). What would have otherwise been meaningless death became instead the seed of new life. Jesus' prayer for life was answered, not by saving him from the specific suffering, but by enlarging the horizons of that suffering so that it might be life-giving for him and for us. So it is with every Christian prayer for healing: God always uses the prayer to transform the situation into life.

Suffering therefore does not deserve a separate category as one of the body languages of the Christian. It belongs to the category of *healing*. For suffering is not, as it is sometimes masochistically exalted to be, something holy and sacred in itself. Jesus came precisely to take it away (Matt. 8:16). It can glorify the Father only by being the occasion for him to give life—which he always does when we pray for healing—either by healing the sufferer who approaches in faith, or by mysteriously using the very suffering, as he did the Passion of Jesus, to bring life to those who need it more.

But we may be more willing to resign ourselves to the inevitable than Jesus was. We may be more willing than Jesus was to try to predetermine the Father to using our pain redemptively instead of asking him to deliver us from it. But it is for the Father, not for us, to determine how to give life. Jesus' example shows us he wants us to ask for life as *we see life*, and thus to ask for specific healing or deliverance. For more often than we are willing to imagine, the life he wishes to give is healing deliverance *here* and *now*. What most often keeps us from asking for physical healing or deliverance is not a mature faith, but a lack of it. For a faith emasculated of risk in the here and now is no faith at all.

To pray for healing in the sense described truly activates our faith. To understand faith as a mere assent to a body of doctrines which the Lord will reward us for believing, can become, if we let it, just an intellectual exercise, if it even is that. It is not costly, and there is little risk involved. But then the Christian faith in its effects differs little from the kind of intellectual or aesthetic faith which the pagans had in the myths of their gods. It entertains rather than converts. The God of the Bible, the God revealed in Jesus Christ, is *power*. Basically this is what the Hebrew name for God, *El*, means. To know God in faith is to touch Power and to be touched by him—and changed. In the Synoptic Gospels, especially in Matthew, we are repeatedly invited to identify ourselves with those who come to Jesus in physical need—the leper, the centurion, the blind man, the Canaanite woman—and to enter into their experience of faith. It is a praying, beseeching, persevering, even pestering faith. And it is the kind of faith that Jesus applauds and answers with his wondrous deeds. And the lives of those touched are never the same thereafter.

The age of miracles is not past. Trained in the scientific methods of scholarship, I have learned to yield my convictions only to evidence. But I have seen the Lord cure before my very eyes. During a retreat that I was preaching in Miami, Florida in January, 1972, a man in his sixties, completely deaf in his left ear and half-deaf in his right, received a complete restoration of the hearing he had lost twenty-five years earlier. No magic, no auto-suggestion, just the power of the Lord Jesus tapped by the faith of a community that was not afraid to ask.

FASTING

again, the work of the spirit is like the inspired melody; it does not reach its fullest meaning the words are put to it.

Finally, a meditation on Christian body language would not be complete without a word about fasting. The practice of fasting is commended by many reasons. Many non-Christians do it, and in the Christian tradition it goes all the way back to the Old Testament. The disciples of John the Baptist fasted, and the Pharisee pointed to the fact that he fasted twice a week (Luke 18:12). But the specific Christian reason for fasting is given, not only in Jesus' long period of fasting before beginning his public ministry but in the fact that fasting bespeaks on the Church's part a waiting for his coming:

> Now John's disciples and the pharisees were fasting; and the people came and said to him, "Why do John's disciples and the disciples of the Pharisees fast, but your disciples do not fast?" And Jesus said to them "Can the wedding guests fast while the bridegroom is with them? As long as they have the bridegroom with them, they cannot fast. The days will come, when the bridegroom is taken away from them, and then they will fast in that day." (Mark 2:18-20)

If Jesus promises his presence wherever two or more are gathered in his name (Matt. 18:20), there is also a dimension in which he is absent, for we do not yet see him face to face (1 Cor. 13:12). The Church awaits her Lord's return. Fasting is a sign, precisely, that she is waiting for that moment of fulfillment and celebration. Everyone would be surprised by a housewife whose husband returns from work only in the evening if she prepared the main meal with all its trimmings at noon and sat down to enjoy it by herself, leaving only some lunch meat for her husband when he returned. Instead, the wife will merely snack at lunch and prepare full festivity to share with her husband on his return. So likewise with the bride of Christ. Whatever ascetical value fasting may have in itself, its purpose in the Christian experience is not to achieve a self-centered perfection, but rather to express longing for the Lord's return. It is a sign to herself and to the world of her faith and hope in his coming.

Back in the days of compulsory fast during Lent, I accepted the practice without really appreciating its intrinsic value. Consequently, my observance of it was legalistically marginal. When Alphonsus Liguori's prescription of "two ounces in the morning, eight in the evening, and only one full meal" was relaxed to the rule of "one full meal, and the other two should not equal a full meal," I remember joking that if I had any scruples about eating too much at the secondary meals, I could always correct the situation by simply eating proportionately more at the main meal. And so, when the fasting legislation was lifted almost completely, I ceased to fast. So it was for several years.

But in recent times I have come to understand in a new way the meaning of fasting as a body language of the Spirit. I was feeling the burden of my human inability to bring about a renewal of faith in some of my brothers. And I felt that the Lord was calling me to fast for them. And so, with all kinds of formless fears about whether I would be able to survive, I undertook a fast and took nothing but liquids. As I anticipated, my stomach growled, and I could literally feel it shrinking as its wall reached inward for something substantial to consume. But I did not find myself with less physical energy, for I did a good deal of manual work that day, and my mind was much clearer to think and write. Above all, I discovered that it began to release in me in a new way what I would call the passion of the Spirit. I began to understand why Gandhi's passion for peace only increased as he fasted, and why Cesar Chavez's passion for justice grew ever more powerful as the days of his fast wore on. And I began to glimpse what a real passion for the coming of the kingdom might be in my life if I could learn the language of fasting. As a matter of fact, I began to realize that this little practice of doing without some food alerted me to a much broader question about myself and my community: "How much do I allow my emptiness for the Lord to remain an emptiness for *him,* and how much do I try to fill it up with all kinds of things that are not the Lord and do not really satisfy? In short, how much do I really long for his coming?"

But if fasting is a language of the body, then it should in some way relate me with others, for that is what Christian bodiliness means. Well, I discovered that too. That night, after a day's fasting, I slept less because I was periodically awakened by the experience of hunger. It was the first time in my life that I had really experienced hunger that way. And then it occurred to me in a very real way, that this is the normal experience of over half of my fellow men throughout the world. Then the hungry masses of India and the hungry children of our own ghettos would not leave my mind. The feeling of hunger was very uncomfortable, but I would not have traded that experience of brotherhood with the hungry and the starving for anything else in the world. I *need* fasting, if for no other reason than to make me painfully aware of my hungry brothers throughout the world.

I found, too, that one of the intentions for which I had been praying for a long time without much success, suddenly was answered that evening in a way that utterly amazed me. I came to realize that the less well attested text of Mark 9:29, which concludes the story of Jesus' cure of the epileptic boy after his disciples' failure, is the one which best corresponds to Christian experience: "And he said to them, 'This kind cannot be driven out by anything but prayer *and fasting.*'"

Opening us to the Lord, fasting sharpens our powers to listen to him and to the members of his body. I had begun to realize this as I experienced in prayer a greater awareness of the Word on days when I would fast. Then I met the wife of a pediatrician, mother of seven children, who mentioned in passing that she fasts all of Holy Week.

"You mean you just eat less?" I pressed her.

"No, I don't eat anything, just drink water and maybe a tiny bit of fruit juice. Of course I break the fast to eat the Paschal meal on Holy Thursday."

I could hardly understand how she could do it and manage her beautiful family.

"Oh, it does me a lot of good. You see, I'm a very oral person. I like to eat and I like to talk. When I don't eat, I don't feel like talking and so I listen."

Stunned by the simplicity of her words, I could only recall the Scripture, "Not by bread alone . . ."

These languages of witness, service, healing, and fasting, are not just body languages. They are languages of that body which is also moved by the Spirit. The body without the Spirit has the advantages only of a corpse— manageable but dead. Even the Christian who witnesses, serves, heals, and fasts must be alert to discern the spirit behind his actions, since there is a zeal that does not come from the Lord. "Test everything," says Paul (1 Thess. 5:21). To think, on the other hand, that we can attain the God who is Spirit by ignoring the body and its multiple languages, is to choose spiritual schizophrenia. The history of Christian experience from the earliest centuries should warn us that such one-sided spirituality most often results in a free reign of the flesh—the greatest deception of the tempter. Body, soul, and spirit are not autonomous parts. Growth in the life of the resurrection is in the spiritualizing of the body and the embodying of the Spirit. Holiness is wholeness.

CHAPTER SEVEN

Mary and Learning the Ways of the Spirit

To know the Lord in the Spirit is an experience. It cannot be learned by the intellectual digestion of ideas, however beautiful or profound. Nor can it be learned by a discipline of will-acts commanded from a control-center. Paul himself said long ago that the Gospel is not something that is acquired by human learning; it comes through a revelation of Jesus Christ (Gal. 1:11-12). Mystery is apprehended; it is not comprehended. He who contemplates mystery does not possess it, but is possessed by it. The charismatic gifts plunge us into the dynamic of this mystery and lead us to grow in the awareness that the life we experience was there before us and goes beyond us. They teach us how to swim in the deep.

In the Lord's plan, however, growth and the growth-ministering gifts are a community matter. We learn from one another and we are disposed by the witness and example of one another to yield to the Spirit of Jesus. If the Christian life were simply a private illumination by the Spirit, there would be no need for a community, and there would have been no need, for that matter, for Jesus. The fact is, however, that the Pentecost Spirit was given only as the culmination of a process in which the life and the example of Jesus were the necessary fore-runners. And once the Spirit was given, the earthly life of Jesus, far from being cast aside, became the model used by the Spirit to fashion other sons like the First-born. That is why the summit of the literary activity of the early Church was the Gospels, whereby the Church read the meaning of her own life in the life and word of Jesus. To contemplate Jesus is then to cooperate most effectively with the work of the Spirit: "Learn from me," Jesus said. "I have given you an example" (Matt. 11:29; John 13:15).

For God to incarnate was to reveal, but it was also to limit. Jesus lived only in one little country of the world, in a span of a few short years. He was born in a given village and not in another; he died in Jerusalem and not anywhere else. He spoke only Aramaic and Hebrew, perhaps a little Greek and maybe a word or two of Latin. but that was all. Such were the limitations of the Incarnation.

And one of the further limitations freely entered into was the fact that being a man he could not in himself embody the feminine polarity in the way in which a woman could. Far from begrudging this limitation, he used it creatively and gave an important place to women in his ministry. And the reason was not merely that women had a right to be saved equally with men, but rather that the community he came to establish in the world needed both to reflect the wholeness of the new creation.

It was not, however, that Jesus was to be a model for the men and Mary for the women—or at least, it was not limited to that. Jesus is the universal model for every Christian; Mary the universal model for every believer.

Why more than one model? Simply because Jesus cannot embody *response* to Jesus, any more than Mary can be the gift to which she is responding. The Christian experience, whether we speak of it in its Old Testament forerunners or in Jesus or in Mary or in the Church is essentially an experience of relationship. The Lord is the God of Abraham, of Isaac, and of Jacob (Exod. 3:6). That is, he can be learned from the life experience of these men. Thus too from Jesus we learn who God is: when we reach the core of Jesus' person, we find him pointing us to his Father (John 14:9). And when we enter into the experience of Mary, we find it totally defined in terms of all that comes to her in Jesus. Accepting Mary as model becomes a problem only if we negate that otherness which Christianity is all about. And thus the Church comes to know what the Christian experience means when it sees it reflected in one of its own, Mary. From Luke and John we can conclude that we are to learn from her two basic aspects of the Christian life: faith in the Lord's word and docility to the Holy Spirit.

Mary's faith stands out especially when we consider the relation of faith to signs. "Show us a sign and we will believe," the leaders said to Jesus. And Jesus' response was basically this: "If you believe, you will see signs. If you do not believe, you will see no sign at all." John summarizes the results of Jesus' public ministry with these somber words: "Though he had done so many signs before them, yet they did not believe in him" (John 12:37). No number of signs will produce faith in him who is not disposed to believe. For the disciple, however, one sign is sufficient: "This, the first of his signs, Jesus did at Cana in Galilee . . . and his disciples believed in him" (John 2:11). But in that very Cana incident there was a faith that believed with no sign at all, and it was the faith that won the miracle: the faith of Mary.

Even Zachary, depicted by Luke as the ideal Jew, "righteous before God, walking in all the commandments and ordinances of the Lord blameless" (Luke 1:-6), showed the kind of faith that needed a sign. He got a negative one, the loss of speech. Mary had the kind of faith that did not need a sign, nor did it ask for one, but she was given one, the news of her cousin's pregnancy. She was proclaimed blessed for having believed, in a way that Zachary had not, that the Lord would do what he had promised (Luke 1:45). She is hailed, in a word from Jesus himself, as blessed for hearing the word of God and keeping it (Luke 11:28), words which immediately precede Jesus' condemnation of his contemporaries who seek a sign from heaven. The only real sign they will see, he tells them, will be the people who have believed the word (Luke 11:29-32). And if the faith of the Ninevites would challenge this disbelieving generation, the intensity of Mary's faith would challenge the weak faith even of believers. Such is the message of Luke.

And such is the message I need. The charismatic experience has led me to discover afresh the power of faith to work wonders. True, signs sometimes precede faith. When I look at my past, I see I have been given multiple signs which have invited me to believe in the Lord's power. These precious moments in my salvation history are moments of exodus, moments of entry into a new land, moments of deliverance. They are grace, all of them. But none of them gives me the right to expect a repetition of them without a renewed faith on my part. For faith is like walking on the water. No matter how much I walk, the water never turns to ice. Signs are an encouragement to faith, but no previous sign and no previous act of faith relieves me of the need of believing *now*, if I would contact the power of the Lord *now*.

It is here that I find the faith of Mary a guide and an encouragement. Unlike the disbelievers, she did not ask first for a sign as the price tag for her faith. She simply believed, and the whole of God's saving power opened before her. Unlike the half-believing disciples who, having seen the multiplication of the loaves, could still complain about lacking bread, she did not merit the rebuke of Jesus, "Do you not yet perceive or understand? Are your hearts hardened? Having eyes do you not see, and having ears do you not hear?" (Mark 8:17-18). Confronted by a similar shortage, she simply addressed Jesus, "They have no wine" (John 2:3). And the new wine flowed in abundance.

And so will it be for me if I can learn to have the kind of faith Mary had.

The charismatic life is one totally surrendered to the Spirit, a life led by the Spirit (Rom. 8:14; Gal. 5:18). How, though, in practice, do I know in what direction the Spirit is leading me? The Lord's word tells me that I need to discern the movements of God's Spirit and to distinguish them from other impulses (1 Thess. 5:-19-21). And it gives me several guidelines for discernment—conformity to sound doctrine (Deut. 13:2-6), conformity to the purest moral standards (1 Thess. 4:-3-8), the fruits that the Spirit bears, especially fraternal love (Matt. 7:16-20; Gal. 5:16-26). But the theologians of the early Church, especially Paul and John, were keenly aware that the Church itself, like the Spirit, has a unified consciousness that transcends prescriptions and even these discerning signs. That is, all of the ethical expectations derived from a much deeper life of the Spirit, which could never be explained as merely the sum total of the ethical expectations. When, for example, the Christian community is called simply "the way" (Acts 9:2; 19:9, 23, etc.), or when it is personified as a woman, as a city, as the mother, as the bride, I am being clearly informed that there is a unifying "Wisdom" in which all derivative consequences are seen as one.

The movement of the Spirit is thus translated in more assimilable light by the deep desire and longing of this woman-type. Thus the invitation of the Spirit is echoed by the invitation of the Church, personified as a woman: "The Spirit and the Bride say, 'Come.'" The Bride's "Come" is the Spirit's "Come" put in her heart, and that "Come" is addressed on the one hand to the Lord Jesus to hasten his return, and, on the other, to the believer to lead him to the waters which will give him the refreshing foretaste of that coming (Rev. 22:-17).

All of this suggests that the Spirit's activity in the individual and in the community is experienced in an intuitive, integral "feminine" receptivity that cannot be fully known in analytical "masculine" ways. The most amazing thing is that the Lord has given his Church not merely a Jungian archetype but a very real person from whom this "intuitive" way can be learned. It is Mary.

With Mary I learn to listen in the Spirit to the Word. I learn above all to wait for the fullness of that word and not to seize too rapidly on that partial aspect of the word which appeals to my impetuousness. If Mary is the model listener, then recalling her can dispose me to the Spirit's action of preparing my heart for the Word.

Mary above all embodies wholeness. Charismatics are

often accused of fanaticism. At times the accusation comes from persons who are not themselves willing to take a life-risk of faith. But sometimes the accusations are true—and it is only because those charismatics did not adequately discern the Spirit. They seized on the partial view and exaggerated it by their own human impetuousness to the point of making a monster of the initial movement of the Spirit. Their way of receiving the Spirit was not whole. It was not balanced. It was not Marian.

The presence of Mary can particularly preserve me from a bitter, an untempered zeal. As mother, she can school me in that love that does not exclude in order to purify but rather embraces in order to redeem.

That is why Mary has so much to offer to anyone or any community claiming the power of Jesus' spirit. Her presence and her wholeness interpret the Spirit in the most wholesome way. As a word takes its meaning from the context in which it appears, so the Word of God takes its meaning from the context in which God chooses to have it appear. That context two thousand years ago was the womb and the heart of Mary. Is there any reason to think it would be different today? Only if the Marian understanding of the word were unavailable to us. But even the New Testament indicates that such an understanding is available, for a physical presence of Mary is no more necessary to us for that understanding than it was to the communities of Luke and John. And yet they had that understanding and knew it was a gift of the Lord.

Finally, Mary has much to tell me about ministry to those who have not yet felt the intense power of the Holy Spirit. One of the greatest frustrations I have experienced is the inability to communicate my experience of the Lord to others. By the Lord's grace, I have felt how easy is his yoke and how light his burden. But many others still seem to experience their own lives as heavily burdened, and it is not surprising, for the resources to which they turn are like the ones I once turned to, human and pedestrian. They do not seem to even grasp the possibility of the Lord really bringing his relief and consolation and healing and power. And so I have often preached to them with frustration and impatience and self-righteousness—which I know is not from the Lord. It is here that I find the example and the presence of Mary helpful. In the upper room she was surrounded by those pedestrian disciples who did not understand what Jesus was all about, who were huddled together with the doors shut in fear, who hardly knew how or what to pray for, and who knew very little even about waiting. She, on the other hand, had, according to Luke, received her personal Pentecost years before. We can hardly imagine that her reaction to the disciples was anything other than maternal love and tenderness, a radiation of the Spirit without a preaching of demands or expectations. She knew how to minister to them in a most loving and gentle way. She knew, above all, to await the moment of God's grace, and she knew that that moment would be hastened not by her impatience but rather by her prayer and her love and her presence. She had waited for nine months to see the fruit of the Spirit in the promised Son. Could she not wait again with the same faith and expectation to see the gift of the Son in the promised Spirit?

The experience of Mary, then, is one of the most precious gifts of the Spirit. She is a charism of the Spirit in person. From her I learn to believe more purely, to discern the Spirit more clearly, to listen to the Word more intently, and to await more creatively the hour of the Lord's coming.

By her being and her vocation, Mary expresses to me the blessing Paul wished for his community: "May God himself, the author of peace, make you holy through and through, and may your whole being, spirit, soul, and body, be preserved blameless for the coming of our Lord Jesus Christ" (1 Thess. 5:23).

Amen. Come, Lord Jesus!

years my prayer life lacked vitality and real communion power. Very little seemed to be happening in my life and it was not for lack of effort. I came to believe